Literature, Autonomy and Commitment

Literature, Autonomy and Commitment

Aukje van Rooden

BLOOMSBURY ACADEMIC
NEW YORK • LONDON • OXFORD • NEW DELHI • SYDNEY

BLOOMSBURY ACADEMIC
Bloomsbury Publishing Inc
1385 Broadway, New York, NY 10018, USA
50 Bedford Square, London, WC1B 3DP, UK

BLOOMSBURY, BLOOMSBURY ACADEMIC and the Diana logo are trademarks of Bloomsbury Publishing Plc

First published in the United States of America 2019
This paperback edition published in 2021

Copyright © Aukje van Rooden, 2015
English translation, Copyright © Aukje van Rooden, 2019

Originally published in Dutch as Aukje van Rooden, *Literatuur, autonomie en engagement. Pleidooi voor een nieuw paradigma*. Amsterdam: Amsterdam University Press, 2015 [ISBN: 978-90-8964-707-8] © Aukje van Rooden / Amsterdam University Press B.V., Amsterdam 2015

All rights reserved by Amsterdam University Press

Cover design by Eleanor Rose
Cover photograph © Getty Images

All rights reserved. No part of this publication may be reproduced or transmitted in any form or by any means, electronic or mechanical, including photocopying, recording, or any information storage or retrieval system, without prior permission in writing from the publishers.

Bloomsbury Publishing Inc does not have any control over, or responsibility for, any third-party websites referred to or in this book. All internet addresses given in this book were correct at the time of going to press. The author and publisher regret any inconvenience caused if addresses have changed or sites have ceased to exist, but can accept no responsibility for any such changes.

Whilst every effort has been made to locate copyright holders the publishers would be grateful to hear from any person(s) not here acknowledged.

Library of Congress Cataloging-in-Publication Data
Names: Rooden, Aukje van, author.
Title: Literature, autonomy and commitment / Aukje van Rooden.
Other titles: Literatuur, autonomie en engagement. English
Description: New York, NY: Bloomsbury Academic / Bloomsbury Publishing Inc., 2019. | "Originally published in Dutch as Literatuur, autonomie en engagement. Pleidooi voor een nieuw paradigm by Amsterdam University Press . . . Amsterdam, the Netherlands." | Includes bibliographical references and index.
Identifiers: LCCN 2019007932 (print) | LCCN 2019015429 (ebook) | ISBN 9781501344749 (ePub) | ISBN 9781501344756 (ePDF) | ISBN 9781501344732 (hardback: alk. paper)
Subjects: LCSH: Literature and society. | Criticism.
Classification: LCC PN51 (ebook) | LCC PN51 .R68613 2019 (print) | DDC 801/.9–dc23
LC record available at https://lccn.loc.gov/2019007932

ISBN: HB: 978-1-5013-4473-2
PB: 978-1-5013-7380-0
ePDF: 978-1-5013-4475-6
eBook: 978-1-5013-4474-9

Typeset by Deanta Global Publishing Services, Chennai, India

To find out more about our authors and books visit www.bloomsbury.com and sign up for our newsletters.

Contents

Preface   vi

Introduction: The Autonomy Debate   1
1 The Romantic Paradigm   23
2 Janus-Faced Modernity   53
3 The Relational Paradigm   83

Notes   119
Bibliography   144
Index   156

Preface

This book is a revised edition of the original Dutch version published in 2015 by Amsterdam University Press. Apart from some minor clarifications and additions that can be found throughout the book, most revisions have been motivated by the change of audience and intend to make the book more accessible to the Anglo-American reader.

Parts of the book were originally written in English and published in preliminary and abridged versions in 'Magnifying *The Mirror and the Lamp*: A Critical Reconsideration of the Abramsian Poetical Model and Its Contribution to the Research of Modern Dutch Literature', *Journal of Dutch Literature* 3.1 (2012): 65–87; 'Reconsidering Literary Autonomy: From an Individual towards a Relational Paradigm', *Journal of the History of Ideas* 76.2 (April 2015): 167–90; and 'Our Engagement with Literature. On Literature as a Way of Being', *Journal of Dutch Literature* 6.1 (2015).

Introduction: The Autonomy Debate

Anti-autonomism

Among all the sirens and alarm bells that accompany twenty-first-century economic, ecological and cultural crises, the steady death knell of literary culture is almost reassuring. For many years now, literary historians and theorists have been proclaiming the decline or imminent death of literature and literary culture.[1] The only reason literature has not died yet, they say, is that the poison coursing through its veins is of the awfully slow kind. In their opinion, therefore, literature's imminent death is not a *natural* one, but the result of an intentional or unintentional act of poisoning.

The cause of this poisoning is generally related to the so-called 'autonomy' (literally: 'self-regulation') that marked the birth of modern literature: its hard-won independence from state, science and church. Although the scope and nature of this literary autonomy has always been a matter of debate, it is beyond question that obtaining autonomy has been constitutive of the development of literature as we know it today. Does this also imply, however, that autonomy is an inalienable aspect of modern literature? This is one of the most urgent issues in contemporary debate.

It is generally agreed that, about two centuries ago, literature's autonomy was the necessary pedestal on which modern literature was able to erect itself, that is, the legitimization needed to emancipate itself from political, scientific and religious discourse. Today, however, many argue that this pedestal has gradually turned into a suffocating millstone around the neck of contemporary writers. In their opinion, the hard-won right to speak autonomously, obtained by literature during eighteenth-century Romanticism, has become self-evident to the contemporary reader. A forced claim to literary autonomy would therefore undermine rather than support the power of literary speech.

A very explicit form of this argument is to be found in the anti-autonomist work of the French literary historian William Marx. Literature's 'present disease', Marx claims in his *L'Adieu à la littérature* (2005, *A Farewell to Literature*), is the 'decline in its social value'.[2] Rather than mourning this decrease, Marx stresses, we must conscientiously investigate how we got to this point. In other words, what caused this present disease? Not surprisingly, then, Marx's book reads like an autopsy report, like a meticulous inquiry of the rings on the dead tree of contemporary literature. The main thesis of the book, indebted to Bourdieu's *Distinction* (1979) and even more so to Sartre's *What Is Literature?* (1947), is relatively simple: 'between the eighteenth and twentieth centuries, European literature underwent a radical transformation: its form, idea, function and mission were all overturned in three subsequent phases' – being those of 'expansion', 'autonomy' and 'devaluation'.[3]

After literature's triumphal progress during the nineteenth century, when literary writers were enthusiastically welcomed as the new high priests of Western culture, its social value has constantly been damaged, according to Marx, and with a fatal persistence: 'Without giving an inch, literature has kept to a fatal path, for about three centuries in a row. Leading from Boileau's sublime, to Barthes's pleasure, and from Voltaire's apotheosis, to the suicide of the author.'[4] In line with the medical metaphor of the fatal disease, Marx suggests that literature is incurably ill because it already bears the germ of its disease from birth. This fatal germ, according to Marx, is the autonomy claimed at literature's birth. It is 'the same power that inflated the bubble and pierced it', he argues.[5] The persuasiveness of his carefully documented literary history largely relies on these metaphors of inevitability. 'A programmed suicide'[6] is another one, as is, this time referring to a law of nature, 'ebb follows flow'.[7]

More generally, the overall ambition to sketch literature's 'evolution' from the eighteenth to the twentieth century already reveals the kind of determinism typical of pessimist historical overviews like Marx's. Marx's main question – 'Expansion, autonomy, devaluation: could this process have turned out any other way?'[8] can therefore only be taken rhetorically. His historically deterministic view does not imply, however, that literature's death is entirely inevitable. Very often, the greatest cultural defeatists prove to be the greatest optimists. A telling example is the writer and former prison doctor Anthony M. Daniels (better known as Theodor Dalrymple), who excels on the one hand at exposing the decay of Western civilization, but on the other hand, unequivocally keeps faith with the humanist values that once founded that civilization.[9]

The determinism of historical studies like these, then, does not imply that everything is lost once and for all, but rather that this loss can only be prevented or overcome by means of a clean break. 'A return to zero', as Marx calls it in his epilogue: 'The evolution of literature would then take the form of a revolution, in the proper sense of the word, of a return to zero, from which a new cycle of transformation can emanate.'[10] According to Marx, this new cycle will only emanate when one accepts the end of what, three centuries ago, gave birth to modern literature: its autonomy. In his own words: 'Before sending the birth announcement cards, we first have to write the obituary.'[11]

The loosely defined New Sincerity movement seems to have a similar strategy. This movement, sustained by the socially engaged work of contemporary writers like David Foster Wallace, Dave Eggers and Jonathan Safran Foer, has, as Jonathan D. Fitzgerald puts it, 'made it unironically cool to care about spirituality, family, neighbors, the environment, and the country'.[12] The terminology of irony versus sincerity, instead of the more European rooted terminology of autonomy versus commitment, is typical of the North American debate of the last decade and ties in with the range of pronouncements of the 'end of irony' after the 9/11 terrorist attacks. The most famous of these pronouncements is no doubt Roger Rosenblatt's *Time* essay, 'The Age of Irony Comes to an End'. 'For some 30 years', Rosenblatt observes, 'the good folks in charge of America's intellectual life have insisted that nothing was to be believed in or taken seriously .... [W]ith a giggle and a *smirk*, our *chattering classes* – our columnists and pop culture makers – declared that detachment and personal whimsy were the necessary tools for an oh-so-cool life.'[13] It is the widely spread cultural attitude of ironic detachment that is believed to have died with the victims of the terrorist attacks and that, according to Rosenblatt and others, should make way for sincere forms of political and social commitment. Again, the birth announcement card of a new form of social commitment is accompanied by the obituary of its counterpart.

More specifically drawing back on the existentialist plea for a *littérature engagée*, New Sincerity scholars argue for a form of literature that clearly roots itself in society, both in its subject matter and in its language use and, in doing so, enables one consciously and actively to engage with the world we live in. In their deliberate and active engagement, these socially committed works would, these scholars hold, finally renounce the detached, self-absorbed and deceivingly ironical literature that in their opinion has dominated the past few decades and that should be traced back to the roots of literary irony in eighteenth-century Romanticism.[14] In contemporary literary theory, this plea for a return to more socially engaged forms of literature is also expressed in terms of 'Post-Postmodernism' or 'Metamodernism' – neologisms that stress even more explicitly than that of 'New Sincerity' the need for a new beginning.[15]

A similar attack on literary disengagement can be found in more reader-oriented studies. In her *Uses of Literature* (2008), as well as in her later book, *The Limits of Critique* (2015), for instance, Rita Felski targets the detached stance that is, since Kant's *Critique of* the *Power of Judgment* (1790), considered essential to the reception of literature: 'Thanks to the institutional entrenchment of negative aesthetics, a spectrum of reader responses has been ruled out of court in literary theory.'[16] Replacing what she calls the 'negative aesthetics' of detachment by a 'positive aesthetics'[17] or 'post-critical reading',[18] Felski aims to delineate modes of engagement that have been overlooked or, even worse, wilfully denied by what she coins literature's age-old 'suspicion' towards society: 'We are called on to adopt poses of analytical detachment, critical vigilance, guarded suspicion; humanities scholars suffer from a terminal case of irony, driven by the uncontrollable urge to put everything in scare quotes.'[19] Echoing William Marx's metaphor of the terminal disease, Felski's aim is to identify the necessary conditions for a new direction, a return to zero indeed, that enables us to regain literature's social value.

Felski finds this new direction in a form of reader response theory. The modes of engagement discussed in *Uses of Literature* and *The Limits of Critique* are therefore not forms of direct political or social action, but rather the cognitive and affective modes of engagement necessary for such a commitment to take place at all: what she identifies in her 2008 book as 'recognition', 'enchantment', 'knowledge' and 'shock'. It is, Felski argues, the 'ingrained Romantic tradition of anti-worldliness' that is to blame for ignoring these cognitive and affective modes of engagement 'in idealizing an autonomous, difficult art as the only source of resistance' to repressive power structures.[20] As did the aforementioned anti-autonomists, Felski blames the Romantic idea of literary autonomy for having led to the disregard of precisely those lay readers' responses that are rooted within everyday society. Her ambition is therefore to bridge this gap between art and society or, as she puts it in *The Limits of Critique*, to build 'a language of *attachment* as robust and refined as our rhetoric of *detachment*', a language that 'depends on [the literary work's, AvR] social embedding rather than being opposed to it'.[21]

Another interesting anti-autonomist contribution to the autonomy debate is that made by Tzvetan Todorov, since he has long been one of the most ardent advocates of the disentanglement of literature from society. Coming from a country where literature was nothing if not a form of social intervention, a radical *apolitical* approach to literature was the only way not to side with or against the dictatorial regime. After having moved from Bulgaria to France, Todorov became one of the leading figures of structuralist and formalist approaches to literature. Looking back on his intellectual development, in his 2007 book *La littérature en péril* (*Literature in Danger*), Todorov concludes to his shame that his apolitical approach to literature has led to a largely disengaged, and possibly even unsocial, form of literature, in the free Western world that is. Like the other anti-autonomist contributions to the debate, Todorov's book, however, is not only sounding the alarm, but also offers a solution.

Todorov suggests a similar hop, skip and a jump as we have seen with Marx and Felski: taking a step back, returning to ground zero, to prepare for the jump over the yawning gap that currently separates literature from the world. 'Literature has a vital role to play', Todorov holds, 'but it is only able to do so when we take it in the strong and inclusive sense that it had in Europe until the end of the nineteenth century and that has now been deprecated.'[22] Similarly, Todorov's more inclusive view of literature again implies overcoming literature's isolation, throwing a bridge to the world. Our present task, Todorov argues, is 'to free literature from the suffocating corset of formal wordplays, nihilist laments and solipsist ventriloquism that fence it in'.[23] Only if literature is freed from these suffocating forms of literary autonomism, Todorov concludes, can we recognize and appreciate the kind of value literature already has for many a non-professional reader: as narrations 'that help people to live better lives'.[24] In her New Formalist work *Forms: Whole, Rhythm, Hierarchy, Network* (2015), Caroline Levine suggests to do just that: freeing literature from the solipsist focus on its formal wordplays. Not by doing away with formalism altogether, but by conceiving of 'forms' in a new way, that is, as arrangements of all sorts determining both literature and social life.[25] The ultimate aim, then, for Levine, too, is to show that literary research '*matters*' and that we 'can learn something from it'.[26]

Although this overview of anti-autonomist interventions to the debate is far from exhaustive, it is safe to say that the general assumption underlying these interventions is that literature can only regain its social relevance when it tightens the bonds with society that it once severed in order to emancipate itself. That is, when it presents the idea of literary autonomy as a Romantic illusion to be shattered in order to reveal literature as an active part of historical reality. All tend to ascribe literature's devaluation to the emergence of a gap between literature and society and all link the emergence of this gap to the fact that literature, since its autonomization around 1800, was allowed to be concerned with itself alone. This autonomization, anti-autonomists claim, enabled literary writers to free themselves from engaging with, and intervening in, society and encouraged them to wallow comfortably in a legitimate form of social isolation. If literature were to 'matter' again, if it were to regain its 'use', 'relevance' or 'sincerity' in contemporary society, to 'help people to live better lives' or, in Marx's words, to be 'lifted to the level of reality',[27] anti-autonomists hold, this isolation needs to be overcome. The main aim of all these anti-autonomist contributions is therefore, in summary, to *bridge* the gap between literature and society.

Against anti-autonomism

Although the concerns about literature's diminishing social role are widely shared, the anti-autonomist view has encountered fierce resistance from defenders of literary autonomy. It may well be that our view on literature is in need of revision, is the objection put forward, but literary autonomy is the inalienable essence of modern literature, and there is no going back on this. Autonomy, they claim, is the very heart of modern literature, its spine, its condition of existence. Abandoning it would not be a chance of direction or a salutary return to zero, but a destruction of literature altogether. If there is any reason to fear literature's death or suffocation, it will not be its autonomous status, but rather its being left at the mercy of market capitalism or politics. According to autonomists, it is not the stubborn preservation of literary autonomy, but rather its reckless renouncement, that will lead to literature's certain death. This is why autonomists see it as their most important task to adjust the eighteenth-century notion of literary autonomy to the present situation, such as we can see, for instance, in the recent studies by Loesberg, Jusdanis and Goldstone.[28]

One of the most devoted defenders of literary autonomy of the past decades, however, is probably Pierre Bourdieu. This may come as a surprise, since Bourdieu is famous for having developed, in *Distinction* (1979) and *Rules of Art* (1992), an approach to literature that seriously downplayed the idea of literary autonomy. Bourdieu's sociological analyses and fieldwork are generally considered to have shattered the age-old illusion of literature being a matter of unselfish, disinterested production and appreciation. The Republic of Letters founded during eighteenth-century Romanticism may well be, Bourdieu holds in *Rules of Art*, a social field with its own specific rules, but this field is far from autonomous. Decisions made in the field of literature have direct repercussions in the economic field, among others, and are, for that very reason, always strategically made. The sociology of literature that Bourdieu delineated in the 1980s and 1990s has, since then, grown into an internationally flourishing branch of literary theory.

The aim of this sociological approach by literature is twofold: on the one hand, it subscribes to the idea of literature having become *socially* autonomous, by meticulously analysing the operations typical of the literary field and its institutions. On the other hand, it invalidates the Romantic claim of *aesthetic* autonomy by disclosing the social, economic and political interests at stake in aesthetic judgements. Notwithstanding his aim to provide a 'social critique of the judgment of taste', as the subtitle of *Distinction* suggests, Bourdieu's use of the word 'critique', however, should not be considered as an all-out attack on the idea of literary autonomy, but as an attempt to *krinein*, that is, to differentiate and analyse this phenomenon in a neutral manner. In other words, for the early Bourdieu, it is not a matter of approving or rejecting literature's autonomy, but of dissecting the way it operates.

It is this pretension of scientific neutrality that the later Bourdieu deliberately drops, if ever there were such a thing. Increasing globalization and aggressively advancing market forces compel us to abandon the neutrality that we mistakenly took for scientific objectivity, he stresses in *Firing Back: Against the Tyranny of the Market 2* (2003).[29] Scientists, philosophers and artists – they should all, according to Bourdieu, fill newspaper columns and television shows to sound the alarm over the imminent loss of cultural values as a result of the tyranny of the market. In this respect, the chapter 'Culture is in Danger' starts with a confession: 'I have often warned against the prophetic temptation … of social scientists to announce … present and future ills. But I find myself led by the logic of my work to exceed the limits I had set for myself in the name of a conception of objectivity that has gradually appeared to me as a form of censorship.'[30] Now that the effects of increasing privatization and globalization are becoming more and more apparent, we can no longer passively sit on the sidelines, according to Bourdieu.

Like the anti-autonomists, Bourdieu is sounding the alarm bell over the imminent loss of (literary) culture and urging us to take up our cudgels. However, his diagnosis of the threat differs radically from that of his colleagues. Indeed, for Bourdieu, the main threat to contemporary cultural products is the *disappearance* of their autonomy. This disappearance, he stresses, is not the result of an inevitable historical process. 'I have always stressed the fact that this process [of autonomisation, AvR] is not in any sense a linear and teleological development of the Hegelian type and that process toward autonomy could be suddenly interrupted, as we have seen with dictatorial regimes', he argues in the section entitled 'Autonomy Threatened',

> but what is currently happening to the universes of artistic production throughout the developed world is entirely novel and truly without precedent: the hard-won independence of cultural production and circulation from the necessities of economy is being threatened, in its very principle, by the intrusion of commercial logic at every stage of the production and circulation of cultural goods.[31]

According to Bourdieu, literature is currently in danger, not because it has been suffocated in a hermetically sealed-off ivory tower, but because an all-intrusive economic logic has intoxicated the life-giving oxygen so far provided by literature's autonomy.

Although Bourdieu would no doubt be as delighted as many an anti-autonomist if contemporary literature were to conquer the hearts and minds of whole hordes of new readers, he would first suspect that these readers had been being lured by some artificially created consumer's hype. Literature's waning popularity is, in his view, not so much due to the perversion of its autonomy, but to 'a regression from work to product, from authors to engineers or technicians'.[32] Bridging the alleged gap between literature and society will not turn this tide, he maintains, because the only bridge likely to be built by a market-driven society like ours will be the bridge of economic profit. Not surprisingly, today's most successful 'cultural' products, Bourdieu observes, are consumer's products in disguise.[33]

This does not alter the fact that Bourdieu, too, calls for a more active participation of writers in society to counter literature's marginalization. However, he maintains, that they have to enter the public domain first and foremost *as writers*, that is, with due regard, for instance, to their 'independence from worldly interests'.[34] Again, Bourdieu stresses that this independence should in no way be conceived of as the 'neutrality' of the so-called ivory tower of literature.[35] The existence of such a tower has always been an illusion, and those who believed they were able to ensconce themselves in it – indeed – do need a wake-up call.

What does it look like, however, when a writer enters the public sphere *as a writer*? 'Culture is in Danger' is not very explicit about it. It is clear, however, that the answer to that question lies in a defence of literary autonomy: 'The position of the most autonomous cultural producers, who are gradually stripped of their means of production and especially of distribution, has never been so threatened and so weak'. Bourdieu once again summarizes his diagnosis, in order to continue: 'But it has also never been so rare, useful, and precious. Oddly, the "purest", most disinterested, most "formal" producers of culture thus find themselves ... at the forefront of the struggle for the defense of the highest values of humanity.'[36]

This struggle is the main theme of another essay in *Firing Back 2*, entitled 'For a Scholarship with Commitment'. What we need, Bourdieu argues here, are scientists, artists and writers that form an 'autonomous collective intellectual'[37] and who, in doing so, are able not only to reveal what is wrong in present-day society, but also to open up new perspectives. Since today's politics are marked by what Bourdieu calls a *'policy of depoliticization'* outsourcing political decision-making to economists, a better society can only be reached by first of all *restoring* politics.[38] Writers can play a pivotal role in this restoration: 'The unique and irreplaceable role that writers and artists can play ... in the new manner of doing politics that needs to be invented [is] to give *symbolic force*, by way of artistic form, to critical ideas and analyses.' For Bourdieu, this symbolic force may, for instance, consist of giving 'a *visible and sensible* form to the *invisible but scientifically predictable* consequences of political measures inspired by neoliberal ideology.'[39]

Bourdieu's defence of autonomy in times of distress is reminiscent of Adorno's aesthetic theory, not surprisingly one of the most important contemporary pleas for literary autonomy. The ideal writer, as described by Bourdieu, the writer who would give a visible form to invisible social structures, is already discerned by Adorno in Kafka. As is highlighted by Adorno, stories like *The Metamorphosis* and *In the Penal Colony* indeed clarify certain social structures through their literary form. The social issue central to Kafka's work, Adorno maintains, is the specific way in which positivism and myth are combined in what he calls social 'enchantment'.[40] This enchantment cannot be described or identified as such: the only thing literature can do is to make recognizable, by means of its style and form, the way it operates.[41] Social enchantment becomes aesthetic appearance, is how Adorno summarizes Kafka's merit. The fact that *literary* means are needed here instead of, for instance, scientific or journalistic ones, is, in Adorno's view, due to the fact that the social reality questioned by them is itself to a large extent an abstract construction.[42]

Adorno further argues that this literary power of sensible suggestion and form can only be employed in an autonomous literature that has freed itself from society. Although art forms can no doubt be traced back to socially embedded ritualistic practices, they only emerged as art, Adorno maintains, when they *stopped* being ritualistic practices; a process that according to him is irreversible: '[art] is defined by its relation to what it is not'.[43] This antithetical position of literature does not mean, however, that it is by definition anti-social or socially irrelevant. On the contrary. By refusing to comply with the norms and rules of social benefit, the mere existence of art is already a form of social critique.[44] In other words: literature's social function resides in its autonomy. Or, as Adorno has it: 'art becomes social by its opposition to society, and it occupies this position only as autonomous art.'[45]

The double character ascribed by Adorno to the work of art and that forms the essence of his aesthetics is now specified in a crucial way. According to Adorno, the double character consists of the fact that a literary work is at the same time autonomous *and* a social fact.[46] Because of this twofold nature, literature finds itself on a gradual scale stretched between two extremes: on the one hand, the perverted form of autonomy typical of the empty play of kitsch and, on the other hand, the flat realism typical of, for instance, tendentious socialist literature.

Virtually everyone in the autonomy debate agrees that literature needs to find the right balance between these two extremes. Nevertheless, Adorno's aesthetic theory goes one step further, by claiming that this balancing act is only possible because it is the pole of autonomy that tightens the rope on which literature is balancing: 'Art's double character as both autonomous and *fait social* is incessantly reproduced on the level of its autonomy.'[47] This is not only to say that literature exists merely by the grace of both poles – autonomy and sociality – but also that literature will *stop* existing as soon as the autonomy pole disappears.

Similar claims can be heard from contemporary scholars and writers. Since, in the English-speaking world, these claims are mostly voiced in the context of the New Sincerity or Post-Postmodernism debate, literature's independence from society is not so much defended in terms of its autonomy, but in terms of its necessary ironic, insincere or unreliable nature. One of the most pronounced versions of this claim can be found in R. Jay Magill's 2012 book *Sincerity*. Quoting Adorno in the motto preceding his epilogue, Magill concludes: 'Imagine a world where everyone was sincere all the time … . This perfectly sincere world would have no literature, of course, because literature is a pretend reality. No comedy, irony, or sarcasm, because they all function by not saying directly what they mean or require that someone is caught unawares.'[48] Like Adorno and Bourdieu, Magill is presenting literature's exceptional status in society as the *condition of possibility* for there to be something like literature at all. In other words, in his view, literature's indirectness or insincerity – or, as others would have it, its irony, unreliability, irresponsibility or self-reflexivity – makes up for its inalienable essence and cannot be done away with without doing away with literature altogether.

In twenty-first-century scholarly criticism, we see numerous attempts to understand the social relevance of literature as *proceeding from* this insincerity. The edited volume *Narrative Unreliability in the Twentieth-Century First-Person Novel* (2008), for instance, gathers scholars who try to delineate the ethical, social or epistemological value of unreliability in a range of different authors varying from Vladimir Nabokov, via Kazuo Ishiguro to Dave Eggers.[49] The shared claim of theses attempts may best be summarized by saying that, in the literature of the past century, the exposition of unreliability itself has become a particular mode of sincerity.[50]

A similar claim can be found in the edited volume *The Rhetoric of Sincerity* (2009). 'Sincerity', the editors and contributors to this volume maintain, 'consists of a *performance* [and therefore, AvR] implies a special focus on the theatricality of sincerity.'[51] Instead of, or apart from, being a specific quality of the literary author, sincerity, according to these scholars, is thus something that has to be *performed*, and that is therefore, one could say, in a way always pretended. A 2018 retrospective therefore rightly claims that twenty-first-century scholarship aims to find a 'delicate balance' in the simultaneous use of irony and sincerity, a balance that 'demands sincerity in order to question and challenge irony, while requiring irony to illuminate the exact nature of sincerity and its ethical, ideological and socio-political ramifications.'[52] In brief, this means that the potential social relevance of sincere literature is not only believed to be *threatened by*, but also *dependent on* the ironic rhetorical possibilities obtained by literature after its eighteenth-century Romantic autonomization. Condition of possibility or obstacle? This is the question that fundamentally divides present-day debates about literature, autonomy and commitment.

Tug-of-war

This tug-of-war between autonomists and anti-autonomists is not a recent phenomenon. It has been, as I will argue in this book, the driving force behind the greater part of post-Romantic debates in literary theory. In his 'Two Cheers for Aesthetic Autonomy' (2005), Gregory Jusdanis makes a somewhat comparable claim. If we 'take a historical step back from the frenzy of the moment', Jusdanis observes, we would see that 'the anti-aesthetic of today is really a footnote to a longer tradition'.[53] 'Poetry (and, by extension, the modern concepts of literature, art, and culture) has always had to confront a suspicious tribunal that either feared its power or condemned it for being powerless.'[54] Jusdanis locates the first instance of this tradition in the confrontation between Plato, who famously expelled the poets for misleading the people, and Aristotle, who made a case for poetry's didactic powers – a confrontation that, according to Jusdanis, has been reiterated to this very day.

Although an overview spanning almost the whole history of mankind might be a bit too sweeping for the purposes of this book, Jusdanis's subsequent claim that this confrontation has 'intensified in modernity … because art has developed into a separate domain of social practice' is certainly insightful in order to understand the recent tug-of-war between autonomists and anti-autonomists. The reason for this intensification, Jusdanis maintains, 'lies in aesthetic autonomy. For when philosophers and artists began to justify art based on its independence from social life, they necessarily exposed art to endless doubts about its validity.'[55] Although the specific details of the current autonomy debate are new, the debate itself is thus but the most recent version of the tug-of-war between autonomism and anti-autonomism dating back to the era of Romanticism.

This shows that deterministic literary histories speaking of an 'evolution' of literature and of a 'progressive disease' conceal the repetitive oscillating movement between defenders of literary autonomy on the one hand and defenders of literary commitment on the other, an oscillation which, as I will show, is reiterated in the case of modern literature, among other things, in the nineteenth-century clash between defenders of *l'art pour l'art* and those of social literature, in the twentieth-century debate between formalism and contextualism and, most recently, in the early-twenty-first-century New Sincerity debate. What is more, this oscillation can often even be discerned *within* the respective poles of this repetitive movement. Within post-modern literary theory, often conceived as the opposite of New Sincerity, one can, for instance, differentiate between more 'ethical' forms of postmodernism and more 'aesthetic' ones.[56] Those who claim that a whole new era of literature is dawning or needed are thus very likely merely to repeat an age-old tug-of-war, relabelling old wine in new bottles. Even a 'dialectic of literature' is presenting, as a form of *progress*, what seems to be an ongoing repetition of the basic theoretical opposition between literary autonomy and literary commitment.

The endless repetition of this debate that finds its source in eighteenth-century Romanticism suggests that we might need something more than a compelling *whodunit* to understand the supposed decline of literature's social value. The fact that literary autonomy is time and again just as vigorously under attack as it is defended is an indication of how central this notion is to the conception of modern literature, and how unavoidable when we want to understand what literature is or should be. At the same time, the endless repetition of the autonomy debate suggests that we have reached an impasse, a point where all possible positions are crystalized and where fundamental debate has degenerated into an idle oscillation between autonomist and anti-autonomist positions.

How do we find a way out of this impasse? According to many autonomists as well as anti-autonomists, the first step towards a solution is meticulously to unravel all possible meanings of the notion of literary autonomy. In his *Aesthetic Theory*, Adorno, as noted above, already distinguishes between perverted and 'good' forms of autonomy. Similarly, Noël Carroll tries to discriminate between the more valuable forms of autonomy and their objectionable excrescences, by suggesting a gradual scale varying from 'mild' to more 'radical' modes of autonomy.[57] Conversely, studies of Tony Bennett and Gregory Jusdanis propose making a categorical distinction between several forms of autonomy, most basically between a social and an aesthetic one, which should not be confused.[58] Another conceptual refinement of the notion of autonomy is made by Andrew Goldstone in his *Fictions of Autonomy* (2013):

> Discussions of literary autonomy have tended to limit themselves to a singular concept of the self-regulating or self-contained artwork. ... My aim here is to argue for treating modernist autonomy as a complex, ramified family of practices, evolving across a transnational literary field. ... The four classes studied in *Fictions of Autonomy* lay out the basic possibilities as a sequence of ever-more extensive claims for literary autonomy.[59]

Similarly, Emmett Stinson, in his *Satirizing Modernism: Aesthetic Autonomy, Romanticism, and the Avant-Garde* (2017), suggests that a distinction should be made between 'three broad approaches to autonomy', while stressing that modernist autonomy is the result of rhetorical strategy rather than of a family of practices.[60] In *A Return to Aesthetics: Autonomy, Indifference, and Postmodernism* (2005), Jonathan Loesberg, for his part, does not so much argue for a further conceptual refinement of the notion of autonomy, but rather for a more refined *reinterpretation* of this notion in the light of eighteenth-century aesthetics.[61]

What all these attempts to unravel the possible meanings of the notion of literary autonomy have in common is the assumption that the current deadlock of the literary debate is caused by a Babel-like *confusion of tongues* that has been mounting up for decades, if not centuries. I will certainly not deny the existence of such a confusion of tongues, and I believe there is much to be gained from a meticulous conceptual unravelling of the notion of literary autonomy and its varying meanings: aestheticism, disinterestedness of the aesthetic judgement, the literary work's self-regulating qualities, the literary field's independence of economic value, or the author's freedom from external constraints, to name just a few.

And yet the reason for the impasse of present-day debate between autonomists and anti-autonomists is, in my view, more fundamental than that and cannot – or can not only – be resolved by means of conceptual refinement. More important than distinguishing between different forms, levels or strategies of autonomy, or between autonomist and anti-autonomist positions to begin with, is understanding what they have in common, discerning what premises they share and from what shared desire or aspiration they spring.

Strikingly, in the aforementioned debates, both the sceptics of literary autonomy and its defenders claim to argue in favour of literature. In other words, time and again it is *in defence of literature* that its autonomy is both attacked and preserved. Time and again, the 'use', 'power' or 'value' of literature has been put forward against its supposedly imminent 'death' or 'illness', and vice versa. Moreover, the urgency to do so, on both the autonomist and the anti-autonomist side, is motivated by a deep-rooted conviction of the social relevance of literature. Whereas anti-autonomists claim that literature helps people to live better lives or contributes to topical debates, autonomists claim that it can reveal invisible social structures and open new perspectives for a better world. When and why, then, have both sides lost their common ground?

Breaking the deadlock

This book attempts to answer this question by analysing the way in which our view on literary autonomy has changed since the emergence of this notion in German Romanticism. Its central thesis will be that the present impasse reached by the debate on literary autonomy is the result of a *theoretical vacuum* that emerged after Romanticism. Whereas, around 1800, Romanticism was *the* paradigm determining the way we should think about literature and its role within society, such a shared paradigm has been lacking since the decline of Romanticism.

I will first outline (Chapter 1: 'The Romantic Paradigm') what I believe to be the essence of the Romantic paradigm. Contrary to the dominant perception, I take this essence to be the pursuit of *individuality* (the in-dividual, undivided) rather than of personal expression. Viewed from the perspective of individuality, what comes to the fore is Romanticism's understanding of the *inextricable bond* between the individual and society, an understanding in which autonomist and anti-autonomist claims are entangled and combined.

I shall subsequently argue (Chapter 2: 'Janus-Faced Modernity') that the decline of the Romantic paradigm did not result in a new paradigm, but in the emergence of two opposing camps that both claim to be part of the Romantic heritage: the autonomist and the anti-autonomist camp. Although many concepts derived from the Romantic paradigm are still playing a key role in our current view of literature, these concepts now seem to lack a clear, comprehensive framework because the foundation on which these concepts were incorporated within a coherent paradigm has gradually slipped away. The result is a theoretical vacuum in which debates about literature are caught in a fruitless and ongoing tug-of-war between the autonomist and the anti-autonomist camps. The unchallenged point of departure of these debates is the supposed opposition between autonomy and heteronomy – an opposition that has obstructed the possibility of a new paradigm emerging.

In the last chapter (Chapter 3: 'The Relational Paradigm'), I shall outline a new paradigm – a paradigm that I will call the *relational paradigm*. The aim of this relational paradigm is to overcome the theoretical vacuum that followed the disappearance of the Romantic paradigm's foundations, by providing a more contemporary framework for the understanding of literature and its role within society. Inspiration for this new paradigm is not taken from literary studies, but rather from *outside* this field, that is, from recent developments in twentieth- and twenty-first-century philosophy.

What these developments in contemporary philosophy have to offer is, as I will show, a specific *ontological* approach that allows us to understand literature as a mode of being rather than as a thing. The need for such an ontological approach lies in what I propose calling the *forgetfulness of literature* in current debates, that is, the forgetfulness of literature's mode of being, resulting from too narrow a focus on its presumed or desired characteristics: autonomous or social, elitist or popular, aesthetic or moral, or a combination of all these. Taking my cue from the ontological approach in the work of Jean-Luc Nancy, among others, I shall suggest that literature should primarily be understood as *a relational mode of being in the world*. Key to this relational view is that it locates the connection between autonomy and commitment, art and life, the artistic and the social, already on the level of literature's mode of existence, that is, *prior to* the emergence of these oppositions, and even prior to the content or effects of literary works.

The intention of this book is thus neither to defend nor to attack the notion of literary autonomy. It instead makes a plea for taking a step back, providing a better view of what the controversy over this notion is about, where it came from, and what view of the social role of literature underlies it. To do this, a more refined historical-conceptual understanding of this notion is needed, that is, a genesis – provided in the first chapter – of the emergence and development of the notion of literary autonomy, as well as of the paradigm that enabled the modern concept of literature to emerge: that of eighteenth-century Romanticism. This genesis will primarily focus on German Romanticism, but will occasionally also touch on the way in which the Romantic paradigm took shape within English and French literary history. It is therefore not so much the *contemporary* debates about Romanticism that form the focus of this book, but a reconstruction, based on a number of influential historical sources, of the way in which the Romantic paradigm has developed over time.

Apart from providing an historical-conceptual approach, the reconstruction of the Romantic paradigm also serves a polemical purpose. That is, it substantiates the claim that the Romantic paradigm is a thing of the past. Unlike many a cultural or literary theorist, I do not wish to argue that we are still enclosed in the Romantic paradigm, that we are still Romantics. As stated, I will argue that the foundations of this paradigm gradually disappeared and have revealed an antagonistic post-Romantic theoretical framework – described in the second chapter – that excluded the possibility of a *new* paradigm being formulated.

Significantly, the new relational paradigm developed in the third chapter does not take as its starting point the opposition of autonomy and heteronomy – an opposition that is intrinsically bound to the eighteenth-century mindset from which it emerged – but starts from the *underlying* aspiration of Romantic aesthetics to overcome this opposition. In doing so, it does not so much propose a completely different view on modern literature, but is rather a reinterpretation, following recent developments in philosophy, of the aspiration that formed its inalienable foundation. An attempt, in other words, to *re-gauge*, from a contemporary perspective, what is and has always been at stake in modern literature: the aspiration to overcome the opposition of autonomy and heteronomy, art and society. Ideas and concepts of late-twentieth- and early-twenty-first-century philosophy will be combined with insights from literary studies, with the aim of contributing to the contemporary debate about literature, autonomy and commitment. In my view, this is the only way to unlock the paralysing deadlock in which this debate has already been trapped for centuries.

1

The Romantic Paradigm

We are all Romantics

Romanticism is undoubtedly one of the most inspiring and most widely studied periods in the relatively young life of modern literature. After all, if one wants to understand anything at all about its adolescence, adulthood or decay, one needs to return to its infancy. Moreover, in the case of modern literature, the childhood years proved to be of exceptional importance. Not only was the newly born literature welcomed with adulation as a Messiah-like prodigy, the great promise of the West, but its grand entrance and tempestuous dissemination over Europe also made for a very compelling story.

It is not easy for literary theorists to keep aloof from the protagonist of that story. Due to its impressive dissemination over the European continent, Romanticism has infiltrated the veins of Western culture, as a result of which it has not only marked one of the pillars of European culture – education – but also resonates in virtually all key concepts of its aesthetic vocabulary. Literary theorists investigating the Romantic era are therefore investigating themselves. We are, in a sense, all Romantics, they say.

This claim is central to a great number of studies dealing with the Romantic period. In *Romanticism: A German Affair* (2014), Rüdiger Safranski stresses that contemporary thought is still largely Romantic: '*Romanticism* is an epoch. *The romantic* is a state of mind not limited to one period. It found its fullest expression in the Romantic epoch, but it does not end with that age; the Romantic exists to the present day.'[1] Similar or even stronger claims can be found in Hugh Honour's *Romanticism*, Frederick C. Beiser's *The Romantic Imperative* and Maarten Doorman's *The Romantic Order*.[2]

What Beiser calls 'the Romantic Imperative', what Doorman calls 'the Romantic Order' or what Safranski simply calls 'the Romantic' – and what I will refer to here as the Romantic paradigm – are all ways of identifying a certain conceptual horizon or framework, similar to the Foucaultian *épistémè* or the Kuhnian paradigm, which during a certain period of time determines how people think, speak and act. The Romantic paradigm that according to the above-mentioned theorists is still ours does not concern the Romantic view on art in the narrow sense, but rather the overall *world view*, the way of thinking that has emerged with Romanticism. It is this world view that is believed to be still ours because it is still present in, for instance, our concept of the nation state, our appreciation of authenticity or our belief in artistic calling.

To these theorists, Romantic aesthetics are thus as close and yet as imperceptible as our own heartbeat. Romantic notions like imagination, creativity and genius are believed to be unavoidable conceptual categories for contemporary thinking about art. Typically, one cannot recognize the *end* of such a paradigm until the paradigm's conceptual framework has been replaced by a new one. Only then is it possible to reach beyond the horizon that had been setting the stage without our awareness of it. It is, in other words, only from the viewpoint of a new reality that the Romantic paradigm can be seen for what it is – a *paradigm* indeed. But to what extent is such a paradigm shift still possible?

Most explicit in this respect is Jacques Rancière's view. Rancière, too, is stressing that the Romantic paradigm forms the basis of our contemporary aesthetics. Consequently, he also asserts the impossibility of this Romantic paradigm being replaced in the near or distant future. According to Rancière, Romantic aesthetics cannot be anything but the *inalienable* basis of our view on art, because it has determined what art is.

Using a notion that is highly reminiscent of Foucault's notion of *épistémè*, Rancière identifies the Romantic paradigm as the 'aesthetic regime'. The fact that he calls the regime founded by the Romantics 'aesthetic' (instead of, for instance, 'Romantic') is significant and shows the inextricable bond he sees between modern aesthetics and Romantic thought. As Rancière argues in *The Politics of Aesthetics: The Distribution of the Sensible* (2004), among others, the aesthetic regime should be distinguished from the so-called 'ethical' and 'representative' regimes. In his view, all three regimes are characterized by a specific 'distribution of the sensible', that is, by a specific conceptual framework that determines the way people think, speak and act.

With Romanticism, Rancière maintains, the ethical and representative regimes have been replaced by the aesthetic regime. Within the ethical regime, firstly, artworks, or rather images more generally, were basically valued in terms of their practical consequences. According to this regime, exemplified most famously by Plato's view on art, a poet might very well draw the most faithful picture of a doctor, but since his poetry will never cure anyone it is considered essentially misleading.[3] It is therefore not surprising that artistic works were generally discredited within the ethical regime. Subsequently, the representative regime conceived of artworks mainly as a means of representing reality. According to the laws of this regime, which was founded, according to Rancière, by Aristotle and continued until Romanticism, works of art should mirror the existing social and political hierarchies, which meant, for instance, that peasants were expected to express themselves in a rude and unsophisticated manner and noblemen in a refined and eloquent way.

According to Rancière, something like art in our modern sense of the word does not emerge until Romanticism: a mode of expression in which essentially everything is allowed. Within the aesthetic regime, *everything* can become art, Rancière stresses. 'Art', in other words, becomes a deliberately undefined concept. Central to the aesthetic regime, therefore, is the experience of the existing distribution of the sensible being 'overturned'.[4] Moreover, Rancière observes, the aesthetic regime emerging with Romanticism prescribes that art *should not* express existing ethical norms or mirror existing socialpolitical structures, because its essence lies precisely in overturning these existing structures. This also means that art should continuously overturn the structures of the aesthetic regime itself. Criticism of the aesthetic regime is therefore always part of the regime itself. In other words, art renews itself without necessitating a regime shift, which implies that in Rancière's view, we do not even need to leave the Romantic paradigm.

As was already briefly stated in the introduction, I take the claim that we are still part of a Romantic paradigm to be not only partially untrue but even risky. I do not deny that we breathe the Romantic spirit, that the Romantic desires have entered our bloodstream, and that our view on literature has been permeated to such an extent by Romantic concepts that it is virtually impossible ever to free ourselves of them. Nevertheless, the following chapters aim to show that the widespread theoretical foundation that had once turned the Romantic view into a *paradigm, regime* or *imperative* was already dropped at the beginning of the nineteenth century. Those who claim that we are still part of the Romantic paradigm do not only prevent us from seeing the harrowing lack of foundation that has been ravaging it ever since, but also block the view of a potential new paradigm.

Moreover, in my view, the absence of a theoretical foundation is the main reason for the present confusion concerning the notion of literary autonomy. Whereas Romanticism offered an overall framework for the understanding of literature and its role within society, such an overall framework has been lacking after Romanticism. Romantic concepts like *Bildung*, creativity, the self-contained work, the poetic genius, continue floating around, but their interconnection is lost. This situation of what I call a 'theoretical vacuum' will be described in the second chapter.

Romanticism as subjective emotional expression

Before focusing on the decline of Romanticism and the theoretical vacuum resulting from it, we need to establish what the Romantic paradigm was all about. This is no easy task. The rich and multifaceted spirits of Romanticism have presented themselves in many different ways, in many different European countries, and few definitions have been debated as strongly as the definition of Romanticism. By and large, however, literary scholars do agree upon one thing, a common trait that is generally reiterated. Within the Romantic paradigm, it is agreed that literature is first and foremost a matter of the *expression of feelings*, that is, the expression of the internal emotional life of the artist. Anti-rationalism, authenticity and spontaneity are the key words here. Accordingly, and apart from a few exceptions, works dealing with Romanticism therefore all have a cover image illustrating some rich internal emotional life: a tableau of untamed nature, a blushing young woman or, in the vast majority of cases, the stormy landscape of Caspar David Friedrich's *Wanderer Above the Sea Fog*. Because of its emphasis on the artist's emotional life, Romanticism is generally contrasted with Enlightenment rationalism, the specific aim of which was to tame emotional life by means of reason.

Using a scholarly vocabulary, we should say that the Romantic view on literature has been predominantly presented as an *expressionist* one. One of the most influential studies in this respect is M. H. Abrams's *The Mirror and the Lamp: Romantic Theory and the Critical Tradition* (1953), which, although not without controversy, it still is a landmark work.[5] Time and again, twentieth- and twenty-first-century scholarly reception of Romanticism emphasizes the issue of *expression* – whether it is considered a form of genius or of recklessness, a moral uplift or an agony.[6]

The reception of Romanticism in terms of poetic expression has particularly accentuated two features: firstly, it has emphasized the *inner life* of the artist. Abrams, for instance, observes: 'In general terms, the central tendency of the expressive theory may be summarised in this way: a work of art is essentially *the internal made external*, resulting from a creative process operating under the impulse of feeling.'[7] According to this view, the literary work has to be thought of as the author's inner self made external, turned inside out. With his description of poetry as 'the spontaneous overflow of powerful feelings', Wordsworth has provided the most concise formulation of these expressive poetics, according to Abrams:

> The metaphor 'overflow', like the equivalent terms in the definitions of Wordsworth's contemporaries – 'expression', 'uttering forth', 'projection' – faces the opposite direction of 'imitation' and indicates that the source of the poem is no longer the external world, but the poet himself. Elements which, once externalized, become the subject matter of the poem are, expressly, the poet's 'feelings'.[8]

Compared to earlier poetics that mainly presented literature as a form of *imitation* or *representation*, the Romantic paradigm would thus mean a turn inwards. Literature would no longer mirror the external world, but would be an opening up of the internal world of the poet. This inward turn is famously described by Abrams as the movement from the *mirror* to the *lamp*. From Romanticism onwards, poets according to Abrams are no longer holding a mirror in the hope of catching the external world; they are now drawing from their most inner self, letting it shine and shedding its unique light on the outside world.

The poet turning inwards is closely related to a second feature generally attributed to Romantic literature: that of its *subjectivism*. The deepest inner self that was believed to be expressed by Romantic literature, would not only be strictly private, but – for that very reason – also unparalleled, unique and resistant to generalization. Or, as Novalis has it: 'The more personal, local, peculiar, of its own time, the nearer it stands to the center of poetry.'[9] 'Romantics believed', Honour therefore argues, 'that they were worth more precisely because they were different from other men.'[10] As a result, the literary work was seen as a totally unique biographical piece of writing, a writing that would not only differ from the writings of other writers, but that would, more radically, also be surprisingly unique to the author itself, springing from the ever-changing inner flow of feelings.

Undoubtedly, this subjectivism found its theoretical basis in the concept of genius which eighteenth-century Romanticism took from Kant. Genius, Kant claims in his *Critique of the Power of Judgment* (1790), is the natural ability to create rules freely and spontaneously instead of following the established ones.[11] Although Kant took much trouble over conceptually distinguishing genius from other types of greater and lesser minds, the concept of genius soon became *the* denominator of the quirky artist.[12]

Over the years, the reception of Romanticism has become more varied, and former scholarly authorities have been complemented or replaced by new ones. Nevertheless, the view that Romanticism has instigated poetics of inwardness and subjectivism is still fairly dominant. The chapter on 'Romanticism' of the 2003 Routledge *Encyclopedia of Literature and Criticism*, for instance, begins by stressing the difficulty of giving an all-encompassing definition of Romanticism, but continues by pointing out that the 'typical form [of British Romanticism, AvR] is *expressionistic*: dealing more with the insides of minds and feelings than with the temporal coherences of narrative.'[13] For many, therefore, Romanticism marks the beginning of a form of literature that is no longer engaged with the outside world or the common good, but that is principally bound to the insides of the artist, its matchless genius, the intangible *je ne sais quoi* of the literary work.

This view is echoed by contemporary sociologists of art. Nathalie Heinich, for instance, argues that the rise of the Romantic artist marked the end of a paradigm of communality. With Romanticism, she observes in *The Glory of Van Gogh* (1996) and *Être écrivain* (2000, *Being a Writer*), the 'regime of *community*' made way for the 'regime of *singularity*'. Whereas in the former regime, art was generally judged by a shared set of values, from Romanticism onwards, artists are, on the contrary, praised for their eccentricity, their non-conformity and even their abnormality. According to Heinich, the most obvious result of this shift from the collective to the singular is to be found in the persona of Van Gogh.[14] The more eccentric the personality of the artist and his work, the more artistic this work is believed to be, is how we could summarize this 'sociology of singularity'.

The pursuit of the undivided

Both the emphasis on inwardness and subjectivism result from the Romantic poetics being framed as poetics of *expression*. Even though inwardness and subjectivity are important features of the Romantic paradigm, I believe that the way this paradigm has been framed in the past few centuries is highly misleading. More specifically, defining the Romantic paradigm – that is, the paradigm constitutive of modern literature – in terms of expression, inwardness and subjectivity, involves the risk of concealing a more fundamental notion of Romanticism that precisely forms the *basis* of these respective notions: that of the *individual*.

By this notion, I do not refer to the process of *individualization* instigated with modernity, but rather to the typically Romantic pursuit of the undivided (*in-dividum*), that is, the pursuit of an indivisible unity. I would like to argue that this pursuit lies at the basis of all varieties of Romanticism, be it the more optimistic utopian form of Romanticism or the so-called 'dark' Romanticism, the quite naïve Romanticism that can be found in Schiller or the more tragic form that can be found in Hölderlin.

This probably somewhat counter-intuitive notion of the undivided expresses the Romantics' deep-rooted desire to overcome contradictions, to unite oppositions and to harmonize heterogeneous elements. And the concealment of this pivotal notion, I would like to claim, is one of the main reasons for the current misconception of the notion of literary autonomy. In what follows, I will therefore attempt to re-write the Romantic paradigm in terms of their pursuit of the individual. In doing so, I will mainly focus on early German Romanticism, as it is not only at the root of European Romanticism but has also provided the theoretical basis of Romanticism as a *paradigmatic* view on the individuality of art, the subject and society.

Above all, it is important to note that the individual does not refer to the *person* of the writer or reader. The individual first and foremost concerns the undivided in a more general sense – an indivisibility that should not only be ascribed to persons, but also, and principally, to everything conceivable. In one of the fragments published in the journal *Athenaeum* (1798–1800), co-edited with his brother August Wilhelm, Friedrich Schlegel puts it as follows: 'Whoever conceives of poetry or philosophy as individuals has a feeling for them.'[15] So, to limit ourselves to poetry, it is not the *poet* that is conceived of as an individual, but poetry itself – which, for the Romantics, includes not only the art of poetry, but creativity in the broadest sense of the word.

But what does it mean to understand poetry as *undivided*? Fragment 116 – generally considered to be *the* programmatic declaration of German Romanticism – might be helpful here. The first part of the quite lengthy fragment reads as follows:

> Romantic poetry is a progressive universal poetry. Its destiny is not merely to reunite all the different genres and to put poetry in touch with philosophy and rhetoric. Romantic poetry wants to and should combine and fuse poetry and prose, genius and criticism, art poetry and nature poetry. It should make poetry lively and sociable, and make life and society poetic. It should poeticize wit and fill all of art's forms with sound material of every kind to form the human soul, to animate it with flights of humor. Romantic poetry embraces everything that is purely poetic, from the greatest art systems, which contain within them still more systems, all the way down to the sigh, the kiss that a poeticizing child breathes out in an artless song.[16]

The question central to this passage is that of the relation between the parts and the whole. Poetry, it is suggested, is the grand unifier: not only does it unite all the different poetic genres, it also combines poetry with other disciplines and life to create one dynamically united whole.

Poetry is particularly suited to playing this unifying role, because of its exceptional status within the dynamic whole: it is at the same time one of the elements to be united *and* what unites all elements. Poetry represents, in other words, both a part and the whole, or, better still, both a part and the aspiration or pursuit of the whole. The Romantics believe poetry to be so powerful that it can ultimately even turn life itself into a work of art, or, as Novalis has famously put it, that it can *romanticize* life. Within the Romantic paradigm, therefore, literature or poetry should be much more than just one poetic genre among others. It should transform *everything* and, in doing so, resolve the distinction between art and life.

In order to do so, poetry should also be more than a mere subjective expression of the inner soul of the poet, more than the unique expression of a unique feeling. The subsequent part of fragment 116 tells us what this 'more' looks like:

> It [Romantic poetry, AvR] alone is able to become a mirror of the entire surrounding world, an image of their age in the same

manner as an epic. And yet it is Romantic poetry which can best glide between the portrayer and what is portrayed, free from all real and ideal interests. On the wings of poetic reflection, it can raise that reflection to a higher power and multiply it in an endless row of mirrors. Romantic poetry is capable of the highest and most comprehensive refinement [*Bildung*, AvR] – not merely from the inside out, but also from the outside in.

Poetry, then, should not only shed an internal light as has been evoked by Abrams's metaphor of the lamp, it *also* has to mirror the outside world. More specifically, literature, in the Romantic paradigm, is a *combination* of a mirror and a lamp, because it brings both the inside out and the outside in.

According to this paradigm, Romantic poets are able to perform this two-way reflection, because they are able to 'glide between portrayer and what is portrayed'. 'Every artist is a *mediator* for all other men', as it is put elsewhere in *Athenaeum*: 'To mediate and to be mediated are the whole higher life of man.'[17] The personal expression of the poet is thus far from merely subjective. This is why Schiller cautions the poet that 'even in poems of which it is said that love, friendship etc., itself guided the poet's brush, he had to begin by becoming a stranger to himself, by *disentangling the object of his enthusiasm from his own individuality*'.[18] In the same vein, Wordsworth wants to preserve himself from mere sentimentalism by stressing the necessary reflective and contemplative dimension of Romantic poetry, which would turn a mere subjective expression of the poet's self into something objective and intellectual. This is why he continues his famous description of poetry as a 'spontaneous overflow of powerful feelings' with the significantly less famous and largely ignored warning, 'But though this be true, poems to which any value can be attached were never produced on any variety of subjects but by a man who, being possessed of *more than usual organic sensibility, had also thought long and deeply*.'[19] Within the

Romantic paradigm, therefore, the truly personal should be at the same time truly universal.

This is exactly what is expressed in the first line of the famous *Athenaeum* fragment 116, a line that can be taken as one of Romanticism's mottos: *Romantic poetry is a progressive universal poetry*. That is, Romantic poetry is not so much confined to a separate domain, but is progressively operative in the world. The concluding parts of the same fragment elaborate on this:

> The Romantic form of poetry is still in the process of becoming. Indeed, that is its true essence, that it is always in the process of becoming and can never be completed. It cannot be exhausted by any theory, and only a divinatory criticism would dare to want to characterize its ideal. Romantic poetry alone is infinite, just as it alone is free and recognizes as its first law that the poetic will submit itself to no other law. The Romantic kind of poetry is the only one which is more than a kind – it is poetry itself. For, in a certain sense, all poetry is or should be Romantic.

The Romantics believe poetry to be an infinite 'process of becoming', because it is not the work itself that is poetic, but the creativity of the poetic act. This is the reason why Lacoue-Labarthe and Nancy in their study of German Romanticism suggest replacing the notion of 'poetry' by the more general notion of *poiesis*, meaning something like 'making' or 'creating': 'The poetic is not so much the work as that which works, not so much the *organon* as that which organises. This is where Romanticism aims at the heart and inmost depths ... of the individual and the System: always *poiesis* or, to give at least an equivalent, always production.'[20] As a result, literature is no longer a separate art form within the Romantic paradigm; it is the creative or productive power itself, the formative force. The end product – the classifiable poem or the finished novel – is not really of importance here, only the creative experience of the writing and reading itself.

The focus on free creativity is reminiscent of the genius mentioned earlier – except that the genius, for the Romantics, is not the eccentric, whimsical outcast as it is popularly received, but the representative of all human beings, the everyman. In other words – and this may come as a surprise – it is not their unique personality that makes the poet undivided or *individual*, but their *universality*. The poet is not an exceptional human being occupying an exceptional place aloof from worldly affairs, but is at the heart of mankind. Or, as Friedrich Schlegel has it in one of his later fragments: 'Artists make mankind an individual .... Artists are the higher organ of the soul where the vital spirits of all external humanity join together, and where inner humanity has its primary sphere of action.'[21] Romanticism seems thus to have radically *democratized* Kant's exclusive notion of the genius. The notion of the individual, in summary, refers rather to the pursuit of unity and connectivity than to the unique inner life of the solitary creative individual.

Revaluation of the social dimension of Romanticism

Apart from Romanticism's supposedly expressionist poetics, it is its supposed relation to Enlightenment rationality that needs to be reconsidered. Even though the Romantic paradigm is in a way the manifestation of unease with the calculative reason of Enlightenment, it is, as we have seen, not *opposing* this calculative reason by an emphasis on emotional expression. For the Romantics, the category of the individual is rather a way of pursuing some sort of wholeness through the fragmentation resulting from Enlightenment rationality. According to them, this wholeness is not to be found at the level of emotional expression, but rather at the level of the harmonious *connection* between reason and emotion. Romanticism, therefore, must be situated *in line* with the Enlightenment instead of opposed to it.

A prototypical expression of this pursuit of wholeness through rationalist fragmentation can be found in Friedrich Schiller's letters *On the Aesthetic Education of Man* (1794–1795) that many consider to be the birth certificate of German Romanticism.[22] The twenty-seven letters, addressed to Schiller's Maecenas, the Danish prince Friedrich Christiaan von Augustenburg, show a clear uneasiness with his own time and are, on the one hand, a passionate indictment of what he takes to be an increasingly inhumane society and, on the other hand, an ambitious impetus to a more humane alternative. The historical setting of the letters is the 1789 French Revolution.

Like his contemporaries, Schiller was initially quite impressed by the French people's power to take command and to shape their own society,[23] but when it became clear that the French Revolution did all but contribute to a more humane society, his admiration soon made way for horror and pessimism. The bloodshed that accompanied the revolution was for Schiller yet another proof of the fact that human beings are still a long way from being able to realize their own potential.

If men were ever to realize the dream of shaping their own society, they will have to handle this potential with care, according to Schiller, and first nourish and cultivate it before they actually start by restructuring social institutions. 'The great consideration', Schiller observes, 'is that physical society in *time* may not cease for an instant while moral society is being formed in *idea*, that for the sake of human dignity its very existence may not be endangered.'[24] Whereas a mechanic can have the wheel run down when repairing the clockwork, a society cannot be stopped so easily. A political revolution is therefore not the best way to change society, Schiller concludes, and it may even be that the whole idea of a revolution should be abandoned altogether. What is needed is evolution or, in Schiller's words, *Bildung*, a transformation 'without harm'.[25]

What should be *gebildet* according to Schiller is primarily the freedom to reason. Kant had already summarized the Enlightenment project in terms of *sapere aude* (dare to think for yourself) and it is this project that is largely embraced by the Romantics.[26] They, too, maintain that modern human beings should free themselves of all the dogmas that have tied them down for centuries and that have prevented them from developing their full potential as human – that is rational – beings. However, as Schiller warns us, these rational capacities are not fully developed yet and the society that enables men to use their reason freely should therefore be carefully prepared. More specifically, modern Western society is even a serious hindrance to developing these rational capacities, as Schiller does not fail to stress in his letters.

Although all kinds of social and cultural transformations have significantly raised the standard of living since the Industrial Revolution, they have also led to a far-reaching differentiation of knowledge and labour that have seriously undermined the unity of pre-industrial society. 'Man grew to be only a fragment', Schiller observes, 'with the monotonous noise of the wheel he drives everlastingly in his ears, he never develops the harmony of his being.'[27] If mankind were indeed to fully develop itself, this 'division of the inner Man' has to be overcome by 'submitting the multiplicity in him to the unity of the ideal'.[28] Here we see how, in the Romantic paradigm, the idea of the *individual* or *undivided* is offered as a solution to the undesirable and perverted *individualization* resulting from industrialization and the division of labour.

According to Schiller, it is *art* that is most successful in countering the lamentable division of mankind. Not surprisingly then, the main message of Schiller's letters is that human beings first need an *aesthetic education* before they can even think of reshaping society according to their own rationality. This aesthetic education does not simply consist of the production or reception of artworks, because singular aesthetic experiences would, according to Schiller, only show 'isolated situations of individual human beings, but never humanity'.[29]

Behind or beneath these individual aesthetic experiences, we have to search for something more permanent and durable, Schiller argues, something like the universal unity of the human being: 'Man conceived in his perfection would ... be the constant unity which, amidst the tides of change, remains eternally the same.'[30] Somewhat surprisingly given the Romantics' secular Enlightenment background, Schiller is inclined to describe this unity as 'divine'. In his view, human beings are aesthetically educated because they are 'to turn outward everything internal, and give form to everything external' – two tasks that 'considered in their supreme fulfillment, lead back to the conception of divinity'.[31]

Once again, we see how Romantic art is believed to mediate between the personal and the universal, to draw the universal *from* the internal and vice versa and, in doing so, constitutes the individual *as* a universal unity. If divine power is to be attributed to the artist, therefore, it is not exactly that of an artist-king being the lord of his creations, as many theories about artistic subjectivity have it, but that of the power to express the divinity that resides in human beings as such, in every human being, a divinity that springs from our potential as human beings but that at the same time resolves the singular human being into a more encompassing whole.

This divinity is expressed in what Schiller, in the fourteenth letter, calls the 'play drive'. His view of aesthetic education as a necessary step towards the constitution of an ideal society now receives an anthropological underpinning that is heavily inspired by the eighteenth-century belief that human drives needed to be tamed by reason. Human beings, it was believed, are internally torn between the lower, animalistic drives on the one hand – called 'material drives' by Schiller – and rational or moral drives on the other – called 'formal drives' by Schiller.[32] Schiller deems it impossible for human beings who are still torn between these two drives to let rationality and morality prevail at all times, as his criticism of the French Revolution already showed. They must first practice the interplay between these two drives, ideally in a safely confined area open to experimentation.

This safely confined area is found by Schiller in the realm of the arts, enabling man to experiment freely with the connection between material and formal drives without this experiment having immediate, and possibly harmful, effects on society. According to Schiller, art cultivates the play drive, the so-called 'third drive' that consists of the free interplay between the other two. Human beings are neither merely material or merely rational, Schiller argues, and a fully developed human being should therefore combine the best of both: real freedom, in other words, 'first arises when Man is complete, and *both* his fundamental impulses have developed; it must therefore be lacking so long as he is incomplete, and one of the two impulses is excluded'.[33]

According to Schiller, both an unabridged subjection to reason, as was aspired to by industrialized and rationalized Enlightenment society, and an unabridged subjection to passion, as the dominant reception of Romanticism has it, will deprive human beings of their humanity.[34] Whereas both of these options will in the end only fragmentize mankind, art, on the other hand, is what 'brings back this condition of limitation to an absolute and makes of Man a whole, complete in himself', that is undivided, an *in-dividual*.[35]

Romanticism and literary autonomy

When we wrap up our exploration of the category of the individual within the Romantic paradigm, we can conclude that it is at least operative at three highly interrelated levels: the artist, the art work and society, the interrelation of which is precisely key to the pursuit of the undivided. But where do we locate the idea of literary autonomy within this constellation? This question leads us back to Kant, the most immediate source of inspiration for the German Romantics.[36] It is even fair to say that Kant's *Critique of the Power of Judgment* (1790) has provided the conceptual framework that encompasses virtually all Romantic writings. Kant, then, is not only the most important philosopher of the Enlightenment, but is also at the basis of Romanticism.

The fact that both Enlightenment and Romanticism share a basis in Kant's work is already manifest in the aforementioned appeal by Kant to his contemporaries to think for themselves, to free themselves of established dogmas by using their *own* rational capacities – his appeal, in other words, to be *autonomous*. Developing human freedom is therefore only possible according to Kant when human beings enforce *their own* rules upon themselves (*autos* = self; *nomos* = law, norm, principle), when, in other words, they do not obey principles other than their own, such as those provided by political, scientific or religious dogmas.

In his *Critique of Pure Reason* (1781), Kant had already posed the question as to what we can know for sure when we are only allowed to rely on our own capacities in obtaining this knowledge, that is, on our own perception and understanding. Subsequently, the *Critique of Practical Reason* (1788) focused on the question as to how to guide our actions on the basis of this knowledge gained autonomously. How, in other words, to establish some general guideline for our behaviour in society, when our knowledge is necessarily limited and finite? This guideline, Kant concluded, consists of the duty to let ourselves be guided by no other principles than our own. *Autonomy*, for Kant, is thus not only at the basis of knowledge but also of morality.

So how, then, can we be so sure that we are guided by our own principles and not – possibly even unconsciously – by physical drives or habitual opinions? How, in other words, do we know that we are capable of something like freedom and autonomy? This is the key question of Kant's *Critique of the Power of Judgment* – although Kant hastens to add that finding an answer to this question is, strictly speaking, impossible.

After all, whether or not something like freedom exists will always be unsure, since freedom is not an object that we can perceive. The existence of freedom is, for Kant, therefore always a regulative idea, a so-called 'postulate' or a presupposition based on what we *can* deduce from our own perceptual and rational capacities.

The way in which these capacities are employed in the *aesthetic* domain is, according to Kant, both telling and promising, and this is where Kant inspires the German Romantics. As the title of his book suggests, Kant focuses mainly on the aesthetic power of judgement, that is, the power to judge a specific object as beautiful. The fact that we can find a specific object beautiful – rather than, for instance, interesting, cleverly made or helpful – proves, in Kant's view, that we can appreciate an object irrespective of the fact that we may learn something from it, whether it can be of any use to us, or whether there is some interest in liking it. The aesthetic judgement of beauty is, in other words, strictly speaking without a goal. When we ask ourselves, for instance, why we appreciate an idyllic brook winding its way through the hills of the Black Forest, we could come up with the explanation that it offers some welcome refreshment after a long walk, or that the rainbow surrounding it teaches us something about the breaking of light, or that we can show off to friends who failed to find this brook. But the only real answer to the question as to *why* we appreciate the brook is the utterly naïve 'just because'.

Kant, then, considers the aesthetic judgement as truly *autonomous* because it is freed of all prejudices, knowledge and interests, and therefore based on nothing other than the subject's sensuous apprehension. On the contrary, a judgement determined on grounds *other* than the faculties of the judging subject himself, Kant argues, 'would be grounded in *heteronomy* and would not, as befits a judgment of taste, be free and grounded in autonomy.'[37] Autonomy is for Kant therefore not a characteristic of the *object*, but of the *judgement on this object*.[38]

Although Kant himself mainly focused on the aesthetic judgement of natural objects like brooks, the Romantics resolutely shift the attention to the arts and, more specifically, to the literary arts. Moreover, being poets, novelists and translators themselves, they do not only want to investigate art from the perspective of those observing and judging these works, but also from the perspective of those who *create* them. In line with Kant, the Romantics stress that the creative subject is a subject whose actions are not grounded in heteronomy but are free and spontaneous. However, they take this idea one step further. According to the Romantics, Kant's philosophy has raised many important questions and has shown the way in which the answers to these questions can be found, but in the end it leaves us empty-handed. It is particularly the question as to whether or not we can have sure knowledge about the existence of human freedom that is dealt with too cautiously by Kant in their view.

For Kant, the autonomy of the aesthetic judgement does indeed provide the *hope* that human beings are free, but strictly speaking, this is all it can provide. It does not *prove* that freedom can actually be realized in a world determined by heteronomous powers. Introducing the category of the individual is, for the Romantics, a way of finding this proof in surmounting the Kantian opposition between autonomy and heteronomy. For the Romantics, who not only observe beautiful landscapes as Kant did, but also passionately apply themselves to creating poems and novels, it almost goes without saying that aesthetic activity not only provides the *hope* of human freedom to exist, but is the actual *realization* of that freedom. Or better still, the poet's autonomous creativity – called 'play drive' by Schiller – is for them both the realization and the promise of a freedom shared by all individuals.

As we have seen, within the framework of Kant's philosophy, aesthetic experience mainly served to make a reasonable case for the fact that autonomy would eventually lead to a harmonious moral society of rational human beings. The aesthetic is conceived by Kant as a bridge between knowledge (the true) and morality (the good) – a bridge, however, that can indeed only be based on 'postulates' and 'hopes' and is therefore, strictly speaking, floating in the air. We can say that with their firm belief in the aesthetic experience, the Romantics take up the task of actually *building* the bridge between the autonomous subject and society. No more reservations, time to set to work, seems to be their adage. Or, as Friedrich Schlegel has it in one of his first fragments: 'Kant introduced the concept of the negative into philosophy. Wouldn't it be worthwhile trying now to introduce the concept of the positive into philosophy as well?'[39]

Instead of overestimating the importance of the gap between autonomy and heteronomy, or, if you like, between freedom and determination, morality and nature, the Romantics take as their starting point the *connection* between the two poles in the aesthetic experience. This connection is the most important building block of the aesthetic *Bildung* aspired to by the Romantic paradigm. Whereas Kant's philosophy is dominated by the sceptical 'maybe', the Romantics prefer to stress the optimistic 'almost' of their aesthetic project because, according to them, we are not situated on either side of a gap that might one day be bridged, but we are always already in the middle, where there is no gap to begin with. Or in Friedrich Schlegel's words: 'I'm disappointed at not finding in Kant's family tree of basic concepts the category "almost", a category that has surely accomplished, and spoiled, as much in the world and in literature as any other. In the mind of natural sceptics, it colors all other concepts and perceptions.'[40] As we saw earlier, what the Romantics call 'poetry' is nothing but this bridge mediating between the singular and the universal, a matter of mediating and being mediated.

Organic unity

Obviously, this aesthetic project has its implications for the way in which the literary work is perceived within the Romantic paradigm. Relying on the dominant reception, one would expect the work's individuality to reside in the fact that it is completely self-referential, closed off from the outside world, a uniquely singular expression that can only be comprehended in isolation. Some metaphors used within the Romantic paradigm to describe the literary work – 'microcosm', 'hedgehog', 'germ' – indeed hint at this. These metaphors, however, do not express the isolation of the poetic work from the outside world, but are, once again, a way of underscoring its wholeness, its being-undivided, which in miniature reflects the undividedness of the whole cosmos. The extent to which this wholeness can be achieved is a matter of constant debate within Romanticism, and the early Romantic obsession with the fragment as a poetic genre already indicates that this wholeness is anything but an uncomplicated affair. The absolute wholeness being their uncontested goal, the Romantics nevertheless deem it impossible that it will be ever immediately present in the literary work. The singular literary work is rather only a fragment of a future unity, of a *progressive* universal poetry.[41]

Let us, therefore, take a closer look at the *Athenaeum* fragment that introduces the peculiar zoological metaphor of the hedgehog: 'A fragment, like a miniature work of art, has to be entirely isolated from the surrounding world and be complete in itself like a hedgehog.'[42] At first sight, this description of the poetic work as a hedgehog seems to be a flat contradiction of the earlier definition of poetry as a progressively universal process of becoming. Indeed, poetry that is always in the process of becoming, the essence of which lies in its productivity rather than in its products, can never be complete in itself, nor entirely isolated from the surrounding world.

The solution to this apparent contradiction resides once again in the Romantic notion of the individual or undivided. The fact is, following the logic of the Romantic paradigm, individuality is not only a matter of being undivided, folded back upon itself like a hedgehog, but is also necessarily something shared, a bringing-together of heterogeneous elements. *One is none*, as they say.[43] The completion that Romantic individuality targets is therefore not that of an all-encompassing work making future works redundant. It is rather that of the conjunction and interplay of different works, creating an ongoing dynamic that only hints at an absolute totality. Once again, this totality is not the sum of atomic parts operating within a mechanic constellation, but a dynamic form of connectedness. Being an individual, Friedrich Schlegel emphasizes, is only possible for 'a mind [that] contains within itself simultaneously a plurality of minds and a whole system of persons, and in whose inner being the universe ... has grown to fullness and maturity.'[44]

In this respect, the Romantics prove to be extremely susceptive to the spirit of their age. In the late eighteenth century, the explosive increase in literacy had not only led to an equally explosive expansion of the reading public, but also to that of the number of writers. Supply and demand reached unprecedented heights. From generation to generation, families had revolved around one single book – the Bible – and now suddenly, a generation was born that could nourish itself with an abundant variety of books, books which, the Romantics were all too aware, would be read in rapid succession or simultaneously, or most probably only in part. This was why Friedrich Schlegel, in his *Ideas* fragments, claimed that the individual book 'is actually a system of books'. Although the Romantic work's essence is to be 'an independent work, an individual, a personified idea', he continues to specify that 'no idea is isolated, but is what it is only in combination with all other ideas'.[45] Once more, we see that individuality and society are co-constitutive. Perfect literature, then, is an eternally developing book which would, in Schlegel's view, reveal both humanity and the becoming of that humanity.

If we want to comprehend the full scope of the Romantic category of the individual, we need to turn to one last aspect, that is, the connection of this notion with the Romantic view on *the organic*. As has been said, one of the favourite metaphors used by the Romantics is that of the germ. Just as a germ already bears the full potential of the tree or plant that it will become, the Romantics believed that individuals already bear within themselves the potential for their full realization. Or, as Athenaeum fragment 242 rhetorically puts it: 'Aren't all systems individuals, just as all individuals are systems at least in embryo and tendency? Isn't every real entity historical? Aren't there individuals who contain within themselves whole systems of individuals?'[46] The part–whole relationship that recurs time and time again in the Romantic paradigm finds its clearest articulation in this organic view on individuality.

The Romantics are very explicit in opposing this view of the organic to a more *mechanical* view of the relationship between the part and the whole, a view that according to them is typical of industrialized societies and that sees the part as nothing other than a replaceable cog in the monotonously turning wheel of society. As we have seen, especially in Schiller's letters, it is this mechanization of society that the Romantics hold responsible for the lamentable fragmentation of mankind, for the divided human being that is doomed to hear 'the monotonous noise of the wheel he drives everlastingly in his ears'.[47] Another thorn in the flesh of the Romantics, however, is its apparent opposite: the idea of an harmonious fusion of all the parts into a seamless whole, that is, a mystic communion or, politically speaking, a Hobbesian Leviathan. Not unlike the mechanical society, this harmonious fusion demands of the parts that they abandon their individuality, their undividedness, for the sake of the greater good.

The Romantic ideal, by contrast, is that of a part–whole relationship where the whole is both *more* and *different* from the sum of the parts, that is, in other words, a system, a *sus-tema* in the original sense of the word (*sun* = with, together; *histèmi* = I stand), or better still, an eternally evolving chemical connection of parts.[48] Being the name for the creative, organic power as such, it is poetry that most clearly exemplifies this potential of eternal development. The individual poetic work, therefore, is but a temporal consolidation of this productive power. Writing and reading poetic works, in plural, and more specifically the essentially unlimited genre of the novel, is for the Romantics, as we have seen, not only the best way to cultivate that productive power but, for that very reason, also the first step in the direction of an ideal *aesthetic* society. Because we all bear the germ of this potential, Novalis asserts in his famous aphorism, 'romanticization is nothing other than a qualitative potentization'. The world, then, 'must be romanticized.'[49]

It will be clear by now that this social dimension is implied from the outset in the Romantic view on literature. Literature is the power to build society, we could summarize the Romantic project initiated by Schiller's letters on the aesthetic education of man. Or, better still, it is *only* by means of a poetic power that something like a truly social society is possible. To feed once again upon Schiller's optimism:

> The aesthetic state alone can make [a cultivated society, AvR] actual, since it carries out the will of the whole through the nature of the individual. Though need may drive Man into society and Reason implant social principles in him, Beauty alone can confer on him a *social character*. Taste alone brings harmony to society, because it establishes harmony in the individual.[50]

According to the Romantic paradigm, art, in summary, brings about a harmonization of the human being, that is the condition of possibility of a both truly *social* and *individual* society in the literal sense of the word – undivided, one.

The reception of Romanticism

As can be understood from the above, the Romantic pursuit of the undivided reveals an understanding of individuality that includes a profound appreciation of the relationship between society and the individual as well as of the individual as a society of individuals. Most extensive monographs on Romanticism do acknowledge this intricate connection of individuality and society – or, more precisely, of society *within* individuality – within the Romantic view on art. Yet, it is precisely this intricate connection that is pushed into the background by the focus on what is now generally taken to be the essence of the Romantic paradigm: expression, and, associated with this, inwardness and subjectivity. What was inherited from Romanticism is therefore not its generative complexity, but a simplistic emphasis on art as expression, the inwardness of the aesthetic experience and the subjectivity of the artwork. By re-writing the Romantic paradigm in terms of the individual, I have tried to show that lack of familiarity with this pivotal Romantic notion led to a misjudgement of the social dimension of literature implied in the Romantic paradigm, a misjudgement that is of great influence in the current debate between autonomists and anti-autonomists. After all, both the emphasis on inwardness and that on subjectivity have inspired the concept of autonomy central to current debates: that of a disdainful and unworldly retreat into the proverbial ivory tower.

To sum up, we may state that the emphasis on inwardness and subjectivity is at odds with the Romantic project for two reasons. Firstly, the categorical opposition made in current debates between 'autonomy' on the one hand and 'heteronomy' or 'commitment' on the other conceals the Romantic's attempt to *surmount* this – originally Kantian – opposition. The most candid demonstration of this attempt is probably the virtual absence of the notion of autonomy in Romantic writings. Although the notion is key to Kant's work, it is barely mentioned in the work of the early Romantics, a highly surprising experience for those who have been told time and again that the Romantics are the grandfathers of literary autonomy.

Of course, the absence of the *notion* of autonomy does not necessarily imply the absence of the *idea* expressed by this notion. The associated idea of freedom, for instance, does play a pivotal role in the Romantics' view on art. The fact that the notion itself is absent in their writings, however, suggests that something else is at stake. As we have seen, whereas German idealists such as Kant still took the opposition between autonomy and heteronomy as the point of departure of their philosophical inquiries, Romanticism as a project is marked precisely by the *triumph* over this opposition. By taking the category of the undivided, that is, that of the organically developing individual, as its main point of departure, Romanticism is essentially a movement that challenges every form of dualism.[51] Subsequently, the Romantic paradigm does not place literature in opposition to society – as a means to criticize or to escape it – but conceives it as the realization of a social potential, as the impetus for a better society.

A second reason why the Romantic paradigm is at odds with the current interpretation of literary autonomy is its obvious challenging of the view of literature as a withdrawal from society. The emphasis put on emotional expression, inwardness and subjectivity incites many a literary theorist to interpret literature's sociocultural process of autonomization as a retreat of writers into the depths of their inner souls. The remarkable result of this interpretation is a replacement of the original meaning of autonomy as 'self-regulation' (*autos nomos*) with that of 'disengagement'.[52] Moreover, this semantic replacement made the idea of *engagement* – and not *submission* – the opposite of autonomy. Obviously, this tacit shift in meaning significantly influences the concept of literary autonomy in current debates. The fact that anti-autonomists generally claim autonomous literature to be 'suspicious' of society, adopting 'poses of detachment' and wallowing in 'anti-worldliness', is a case in point.[53]

The confusion of 'autonomy' with 'disengagement' risks concealing what was already central to Kant's claim of autonomy: the critical, emancipatory potential implied in self-regulation. After all, as we have seen, the Kantian appeal to autonomy is an appeal to think for oneself without relying on established dogmas. Conceiving of this autonomous stance as a disdainful elevation above the ordinary man, as is often the case in literary theory, is clearly to miss the point. Indeed, the aim of Schiller's Kantian-inspired aesthetic education, for instance, is not that of an isolated writer taking the moral high ground; it is rather that of a society in which every member elevates themselves by becoming, in a way, a writer.[54]

The eighteenth-century idea of autonomy, in brief, is founded on an utterly social and, if you like, even democratic ideal of emancipation that seems to have nothing of the unworldly retreat to the proverbial ivory tower that has been taken as the main reason for literature's current marginalization by many a literary historian and theorist. As demonstrated, within the Romantic paradigm the truly personal *is* truly social. Since human beings are believed to have the same disposition and capacities, when all obey their *own* law, this law will prove to be the same in all cases.[55]

But where, then, does the current idea of literary autonomy come from? *How* did we end up in the situation where 'literary autonomy' means a withdrawal from the world, an a-social folding back of the text on itself, the creation of an isolated textual world without external reference, a carefully sealed-off textual cocoon, an elitist form of language play? This question will be dealt with in the next chapter. This first chapter's primary goal was to elucidate the most important conceptual category of Romanticism – that of the individual – and in doing so, to shed new light on the roots of modern literature. Moreover, I have wanted to show that this category of the individual invites, not to say urges, us to revise some of the dominant interpretations of the Romantic paradigm, such as the interpretation of Romantic literature as subjective emotional expression, eccentric and a withdrawal from society. As will become clear, these dominant interpretations may partly be explained by an all-too-easy conflation of the social process of autonomization with an aesthetic one. Another part may be explained by the rather one-sided way in which the English and French Romantics have interpreted their German predecessors.[56]

In the next chapter I will claim, however, that the *underlying* reason for both this conflation and this reinterpretation must be sought in the *theoretical vacuum* that emerged after the decline of the Romantic paradigm. Although many concepts derived from the Romantic paradigm are still playing a key role in our current view of literature, these concepts, as has been said earlier, lack a clear, comprehensive framework because the foundation on which these concepts were incorporated within a coherent paradigm has gradually slipped away. Claiming that we are still part of the Romantic paradigm, therefore, does not only prevent us from seeing the theoretical vacuum that emerged after the decline of Romanticism, but is also blocking the view of a potential new paradigm.

2

Janus-Faced Modernity

Unmasking the autonomous subject

United we stand, divided we fall, as they say. Indeed, the Romantic paradigm was not only characterized by an unprecedented expansion of the literary ideal, but also by a remarkable unanimity on the ins and outs of that ideal. Never before had there been so much agreement among the great minds of history. Although Schelling and the Schlegel brothers, Hölderlin and Novalis, would certainly not agree on the detail, they could agree on what they conceived to be the ideal of individuality – whether or not they were sceptical or naïve about the feasibility of achieving that ideal. Rapidly industrializing society, the inspiring optimism of the Enlightenment, increasing mobility and literacy, the vast historical perspective opened up by the French Revolution – no doubt all of these phenomena have contributed to the fact that the Romantics were all touched by the same fire, sensing they were part of a historical *momentum* which was believed to culminate in the ideal society once the intellectual and literary forces were united.

It is this precious unanimity that vanishes into thin air with the decline of the Romantic paradigm. With hopes for a harmonious society having evaporated, the common ground was also fading away – common ground that at that time was undoubtedly already less stable than it seems to be from a contemporary perspective, but that nevertheless provided a remarkably solid basis for the modern view on literature and for modernity as such.

One could say that there are two main reasons why the Romantic paradigm as laid down by early German Romanticism loses its persuasiveness during the nineteenth and twentieth centuries. Both concern fundamental changes in intellectual history in Germany and abroad. The first reason is a gradual but radical shift in the view on the human *subject*. The Enlightenment idea of the subject that was still largely being adopted by the Romantics starts to be criticized and contested from all sides. A second and, to some extent, associated reason is the shift, from the early nineteenth century onwards, in the concept of *truth* in general and literature's valuing of truth in particular. From the early nineteenth century onwards, literature is increasingly conceived of as a matter of *interpretation* rather than of revelation – a change in direction that is already being prepared by the German Romantics, but that is really carried through after Romanticism. In this chapter, I will describe both shifts in brief that marked the decline of the Romantic paradigm.

The initial criticism made of the Enlightenment idea of the human subject is not that of a well-aimed shot, a definite correction, but passes jerkily through a number of influential but mutually divergent theories that all reveal different aspects assumed to be decisive for the constitution of the subject.[1] The point of critique is time and again the Kantian idea of the subject as a self-determining and self-sufficient entity – in summary, the idea of the autonomous subject. Most generally, one could say that the Enlightenment idea of the autonomous subject is first *refined* by the German Romantics, Hegel and Marx, then *criticized* by Freud and Nietzsche, in order to be fully *rejected* by Foucault and other post-structuralists.

We have already seen how the German Romantics aimed to adjust the Kantian idea of the subject in one important respect; by trying to overcome the opposition between autonomy and heteronomy, subject and society. It is Karl Marx, however, who gives the first real blow to the eighteenth-century ideal of the autonomous subject.

Inspired by Hegel's historical-dialectical approach to the subject, Marx develops a historical view of the subject that is instigated by the French Revolution – albeit seemingly leading to a conclusion that is the opposite of that of the German Romantics.

Whereas the German Romantics generally drew courage from the French Revolution, believing it to be the proof of a future realization of human freedom, in Marx it mainly evokes an upsetting form of class-consciousness. Even if reason is taken as our most important guideline, as Marx observes, it is still the reason of a living human being, and this human being finds itself in material circumstances that are not only often unwieldy, but also disastrous for its rational capacities. This does not prevent Marx, however, from subscribing to some form of autonomous subjectivity by projecting the ideal of a classless society: in the end, he believes, oppressive social relations will make way for a truly *equal* realization of human freedom.

With his ideal of the classless society, Marx does not so much criticize the Kantian idea of the autonomous subject as give but another affirmation of it, as Charles Taylor rightly observes. 'As transposed by Hegel and again by Marx, the Kantian aspiration to radical autonomy turns into the idea that human nature is not simply a given, but is to be made over.'[2] Whether one conceives this autonomy as a given, as Kant did, or as something that has to be developed, as did the Romantics, Hegel and Marx, the ideal of the autonomous subject remains in place.

Nevertheless, Marxism has breached the ideal of the autonomous subject in such a way that it is not easily repaired. Marx's emphasis on the subject's material circumstances, on its embeddedness in social classes and on exploitation, did not only urge a social transformation *in favour of* the suppressed subject, but also created a growing awareness of many other forms of possible suppression. Marxism, in other words, opens the full spectrum of possible heteronomous powers, the result of which is that the unbridled optimism of the late nineteenth century starts to give way to theories that lose hope of an ultimate triumph of the autonomous subject.

According to these theories, the subject is thus not straightjacketed by sociopolitical circumstances alone. In the late nineteenth century, the Enlightenment ideal was criticized in the main by Freud and Nietzsche, the former issuing, of course, a clear vote of no-confidence in the autonomous subject with his theory about the unconscious. Human beings may well be under the impression that they are fully in control of their thoughts and behaviour, Freud holds, but in fact they are nothing but a plaything of unconscious drives and desires. Psychoanalysis may help channel these drives and desires, but full control is utterly impossible according to Freud. Nietzsche, for his part, is also inclined to see man as a mere plaything, blinded by the illusion of being able to determine their own fate. In his work on Greek tragedy and Wagner's operas, he even makes a plea, and more strongly so than Freud, for a revaluation of the uncontrollable and the irrational as an essential part of human nature.[3]

In the end, however, the works of both Freud and Nietzsche are a way, too, of investigating the possibilities that still exist for human beings to become autonomous, to free themselves of the yoke of suppression. As Donald E. Hall rightly observes in his *Subjectivity* (2004), in the end both Nietzsche and Freud affirm the Enlightenment ideal of the autonomous subject and, in doing so, provide 'yet another nineteenth-century manifestation of a quasi-self-help philosophy' – a manual for leading a life that is as autonomous as possible.[4]

During the twentieth century, this faith in the autonomous subject is put to an abrupt end. Even though the three so-called 'masters of suspicion'[5] – Marx, Freud and Nietzsche – still propagated some form of the ideal of the autonomous subject, they sowed the seeds of a subject criticism that is now starting to take root. The twentieth century, then, is *the* century of subject criticism. From existentialism (Heidegger, Sartre), to structuralism (De Saussure, Lacan, Barthes) and post-structuralism (Foucault, Deleuze), feminism (Irigaray, Kristeva) and deconstructivism (Lyotard, Derrida, Nancy) – all stress the fundamental and inevitable determination of the subject through, respectively, existential conditions, sociocultural structures, power structures, sexual differences or other hierarchical differences. The idea of the self-determining autonomous subject has proved to be an illusion.[6]

It is especially the work of Foucault that is considered a frontal attack on the Enlightenment ideal of autonomous subjectivity.[7] Subjectivity, Foucault repeats time and again, is but the result of a number of directive and suppressive structures. If we were to take away these structures, the individual itself would disappear, 'like a face drawn in the sand at the edge of the sea', as the famous conclusion of his 'archeology of the human sciences', *The Order of Things*, has it.[8]

One could say that at the end of the twentieth century, the presumably undivided harmonious individual has proven to be a torn, conflict-ridden subject – a highly unstable 'dividual'. This unmasking of the autonomous subject is part of a much wider tendency that can be discerned in the social and medical sciences, but also, for instance, in the novels of Dostoyevsky. As stated earlier, this tendency is that of an increasing awareness of the subject's *Umwelt*, of the context in which the subject is living or, more precisely, of the constant interaction between internal and external factors at stake in the constitution of subjectivity. The human being is no longer believed to hold absolute sway over his environment; instead, a complex dialogue has begun between his inner soul and a variety of external factors.[9]

The hermeneutic turn

Apart from the gradual shift in the view on the subject, another shift causes the Romantic paradigm to fall apart: the change, from the early nineteenth century onwards, in the conception of the *truth-value* of literature. One might call this shift, for lack of a better word, the hermeneutic turn of literature. Although this turn is generally situated after Romanticism, it is in German Romanticism that it finds its roots, more specifically in the work of Friedrich Schleiermacher. The classicist and theologian Schleiermacher is one of the prominent figures of the early Romanticist movement and is not only the first to develop an encompassing hermeneutic theory, but also one of the first to introduce this originally biblical exercise within the domain of literature.[10]

Crucial for the hermeneutic turn is the fact that literature is no longer considered as the expression of a truth *external* to it, but as the kind of expression that escapes the categories of truth and untruth. Although truth is still an important concept for the Romantics, the disconnection of truth and literature is at the centre of their thought. After all, their emphasis on the individuality or undividedness of the poetic challenges a mimetic and referential understanding of literature: the literary work is no longer a representation of nature, but is itself a natural product, an organic whole which is always in the process of becoming. 'What the work reveals has to be read in it', Taylor resumes this new hermeneutic stance.[11] In other words: the 'truth' of literature is no longer something given and to be 'discovered' by the reader, but is something that comes into existence in the process of reading. Reading becomes a matter of interpretation instead of revelation, as we saw earlier, and this literary truth is no longer objectively verifiable.

According to Schleiermacher, the aim of the process of interpretation is to understand the text even better than its author is able to do. In his *Hermeneutics and Criticism* (1819) it says: 'Since we have no direct knowledge of what was in the author's mind, we must try to become aware of many things of which he himself may have been unconscious'.[12] According to Schleiermacher, then, the reader is invited to discern the meaning of a text by fundamentally and personally engaging with the author, which makes of literary truth a two-way interaction modelled on the real-life conversation.

After this hermeneutic turn, poetic truth is no longer a matter of *adequatio*, of the conformity between the literary work and reality, but becomes a matter of interpretation in the broadest sense of the term – of reading, re-reading, reflection, translation and discussion. Friedrich Schlegel's 'Conversation about Poetry' (1800), which appeared in one of the *Athenaeum* issues, is telling in this respect, being not only literally a conversation about poetry, but also a programmatic statement declaring that poetry is essentially conversational.[13] Necessarily, the truth of a conversation is always somewhere in the middle, *between* the interlocutors, as is expressed by the literal meaning of interpretation (*inter* = between; *pretium* = value, price or *prazein* = to point out, to show).

In *Romanticism: A German Affair*, Safranski places the key Romantic notion of *irony* at the heart of this hermeneutic turn. Irony, Safranski maintains, enables conversations, because it helps to evade the dead end of a full understanding.[14] And indeed is irony also a way for Schleiermacher to bring parties closer together without having one of them laying claim to the truth, as he argues in *Toward a Theory of Sociable Conduct* (1799). More important than the outcome of the conversation – that would be nothing but a 'dead end' because it would break contact – is the conversation as such. Or, as Hölderlin has it in the poem 'Celebration of Freedom': 'Since we have been a conversation and have been able to hear from one another' – a line that is later famously taken by Heidegger as the point of departure of his hermeneutical account of the essence of poetry.[15]

Whereas poetic debates until Romanticism mainly revolved around the issue of *by what means* truth would have to be transmitted, poetic truth becomes significantly less evident and univocal after the hermeneutic turn. In this case, too, the one and undivided seems to give way to something more contingent, plural and unstable.¹⁶ As already stated, both changes in Western intellectual history – the shifts in the view of subject and of truth – gradually undermined the theoretical framework developed by Romanticism, that is, the framework that determined the way in which we understand modern literature and its social role.

I would claim that the *possibility* of this undermining is nevertheless already implied in the Romantic paradigm itself. This claim is endorsed by a number of scholars, including Rancière in his 2002 essay 'The Aesthetic Revolution and its Outcomes: Emplotments of Autonomy and Heteronomy'.¹⁷ According to Rancière, the 'original scene' of the Romantic paradigm is to be found in Schiller's letters on the aesthetic education of man and, more precisely, in the fifteenth letter. While elaborating on the aesthetic 'play drive', Schiller argues: '[Man] is only wholly Man when he is playing. This proposition ... will, *I promise you*, support the whole fabric of aesthetic art, and the still more difficult art of living.'¹⁸ This 'I promise you', Rancière rightly states, captures the promise of the whole Romantic project, the promise that the construction of the fabrics of both art and life are the *same*, one encompassing aesthetico-societal fabric in which the unity of the individual would automatically lead to the unity of society.

According to the Romantics – and as we saw they follow Kant herein – this is the promise implied in aesthetic experience. Or as Rancière has it: 'There exists a specific sensory experience – the aesthetic – that holds the promise of both a new world of Art and a new life for individuals and the community.'¹⁹ Although this promise captures the underlying structure of the whole project of modernity, this promise is – and here the Romantics are probably more Kantian than they themselves believed they were – indeed a *wish* rather than a guarantee. After all, if there were indeed the guarantee of redemption, a promise would not have been necessary.

This promise, then, this encouraging 'almost' that the Romantics saw lacking in German idealism, encompasses both the foundation of the Romantic paradigm *and* the possibility of its collapse. The 'burden of speculative aesthetics', is the well-chosen expression used by Jonathan Loesberg.[20] The bond between art and life, as well as their rupture, is concentrated in the simple conjunction of Schiller's 'and'. Rancière therefore concludes: 'In a sense the whole problem [of Romanticism, AvR] lies in a very small preposition. Schiller says that the aesthetic experience will bear the edifice of the art of the beautiful *and* the art of living …. The aesthetic experience is effective inasmuch as it is the experience of this *and*.'[21] The conjunction of art and life is indeed only as effective as the Romantics present it as being, when one assumes, as they do, that the regular citizen is cast in the same mould as the poet.[22]

As soon as this premise is dropped, the whole ingenious edifice collapses. Or, as Tony Bennett has it:

> [Kant's] aesthetic judgment provides for the free subjective harmony between the faculties that is necessary if the other faculties are to perform the legislative roles that Kant assigns them …. The productivity of Kant's transcendental method is properly appreciated *only when* it is historicized as proposing a particular architecture of the person which lays it open to the intervention and exercise of a historically novel form of expertise as a part of the pre-eminently social processes through which bids and counter bids for the regulation of conduct and the ordering of social life vie with one another.[23]

The Romantic paradigm following on from Kant's aesthetics is indeed, as the subtitle of Rancière's essay also suggests, one of an 'emplotment', an entanglement or *mise en intrigue*, of autonomy and heteronomy, an emplotment that has tied art and life for decades but that can just as easily be untied. Although the separate components of the Romantic paradigm were secondary to the ambition to unite them, this dualist understructure surfaces when this ambition starts to fade and when its joints start to erode. Inevitably, then, the links between art and life, the individual and society, the beautiful and the useful and so on, so meticulously constructed by Schiller in his letters *On the Aesthetic Education of Man*, fall apart again in the centuries following on from Romanticism.

Modern duality

This is exactly what happens as a result of the questioning of the Romantic paradigm by the aforementioned shifts in nineteenth and twentieth-century intellectual history. The two sides so ingeniously held together by the Romantic 'and' radically fall apart – their bond is broken. Looking back upon nineteenth and twentieth-century literary history, one may conclude that the coping strategy was not to glue the two parts, in some other and better way, as a new 'individual', but to separate them even more radically.[24] Rather than glue, the crowbar proves to be the main instrument of post-Romanticism.

Within this post-Romantic literary theory, the notion of literary autonomy starts to play a remarkable role. In the attempt to separate the two constitutive sides of the Romantic paradigm, the idea of literary autonomy, as well as the whole notion of 'Romanticism' to begin with, is situated on one side of the newly formed dividing line. From now on, literary debates are debates between defenders and opponents of Romanticism, and thereby between defenders and opponents of literary autonomy, that is, between defenders of 'autonomous' art and those of 'heteronomous' life. After the collapse of the Romantic paradigm, in summary, a *radical separation* of art and life takes place. The intermediate zone that had glued the two sides of the Romantic conjunction together now becomes a closely guarded border. Whereas the Romantic paradigm aimed at a fundamental unification of autonomy and heteronomy, of art and life, the disjunction of this 'emplotment' leads to a relapse into its former oppositional structure. The demarcation line is once again the Kantian chalk, the *krinein* between autonomy and heteronomy that marked his *Critique of the Power of Judgment*.

As a result, criticism of literary autonomy now entails an affirmation of typically Kantian heteronomous elements like use, interest and pleasure. Autonomous literature is automatically considered to be redundant, indifferent and unpleasant. And vice versa, a defence of literary autonomy automatically entails a renouncement of use, interest and pleasure. Non-autonomous literature is for that very reason considered pragmatic, partial or teasing. The dynamics proper to the post-Romantic literary debate, not only in Germany but also and more clearly so in France and Great Britain, are therefore those of an *oscillation* between the poles of autonomy and heteronomy, an oscillation that seems to have no other cause than the mutual repulsion of the two poles. Indeed, we will see how the most important drive in post-Romantic literary debates is to stand up as clearly as possible to the opposite camp.

It is these oscillating dynamics that I explain in terms of a theoretical vacuum. This might come as a surprise, since literary debates in the nineteenth and early twentieth centuries are livelier than ever. Baudelaire and Flaubert are as ardently accused as they are defended, the general cause is as passionately served (think of Zola's *J'accuse*) as it is ignored, and polemic journals shoot up like mushrooms. The driving force behind all these manifestations, however, is not so much an intrinsic motivation to develop one's own poetic position, but rather the extrinsic motivation to separate oneself as far as possible from one's opponents.

Whereas the theoretical framework of the Romantic paradigm functioned as some sort of magnetic field, the power of which was reinforced by the opposing poles, its collapse results in a vacuum in which these poles do nothing but neutralize each other. This is also suggested by Hans Ulrich Gumbrecht: 'I believe that literary studies as a site where intellectual forces combine, risk stagnation for as long as they remain stuck between these two positions, whose contrasts and tensions can cancel each other out.'[25] In other words: the Romantic paradigm is replaced by an antagonistic oscillation that will continue until both poles are incorporated in a new encompassing magnetic field.

Put somewhat differently again, the problem of post-Romantic modernity is that it reverts to a theoretical ground that is intrinsically paradoxical, although both autonomists and anti-autonomists try to do away with this paradox by highlighting one side only. Anti-autonomists, firstly, tend to isolate the *social* character of the arts. If Schiller's letters on the aesthetic education of man do indeed formulate the basis of modern aesthetics, one could say that the anti-autonomists focus primarily on the latter part, that is, on the aesthetic *education of mankind*. This form of modernity identifies art with a realization of human destiny, whether this is moral, capitalist, socialist, communist or other. Early-nineteenth-century French Saint-Simonianism is an expression of this view, as is Russian Futurism or Sartrian Existentialism.

The autonomist form of modernity, instead, focuses primarily on the *aesthetic form* of this human education. This is the modernity of the so-called pure form or style that one can find in all kinds of anti-realist and avant-garde movements propagating some form of *l'art pour l'art*. Contrary to the anti-autonomist form of modernity, these autonomist movements tend to isolate the exceptional nature of the artistic medium. Taking a closer look at some actual cases of the polemics between those two camps in the post-Romantic literary debate will illustrate their unresolvable antagonistic dynamics.

The l'art pour l'art debate

One of the most exemplary moments in this polemic debate is the emergence in early-nineteenth-century France of the *l'art pour l'art* movement.[26] It is an era marked by the rise of the middle class – the *bourgeoisie* – booming industrialization and rapidly changing social relations. As in early German Romanticism, one is still confident that literature is able to form and change society, maybe even more so than ever. After all, with some help from the booming industry, one can easily bend society to one's will.

Because of the opposition reinstated between autonomy and heteronomy, art and life, the question arises, however, as to whether it is autonomist or rather anti-autonomist literature that is best equipped to change society. Two parties are involved in the debate. On the one hand, French Romantics like Victor Cousin, Théophile Gautier, Victor Hugo and Gérard de Nerval, who revert back to the German Romantic heritage and therefore place themselves on the autonomist side of the newly emerged demarcation line – that is, the side of the artistic medium and the aesthetic form. On the other side of that line we find the bourgeois writers and theorists – the representatives of the middle class and supporters of social education – that is, the ones that place themselves on the side of society or, if you like, humanity. These are often writers and theorists who are directly or indirectly inspired by the ideas of Saint-Simon (1760–1825) and are therefore sometimes called Saint-Simonians.

Being one of the founding fathers of State Socialism, Saint-Simon holds an ideal of society that is not at all unrelated to that of the Romantics: a strong, harmonious society where every individual has the freedom to develop themselves. Contrary to the Romantics, however, Saint-Simon conceives of industrialization as serving that ideal rather than threatening it. The transition from a feudal to an industrialized society is for him, therefore, not only an inevitable step to take, but also a very welcome one. Religious and political powers will be no match for the impartial power of industry, he argues, and when everybody contributes according to ability, this industry will be the key to a flourishing and prosperous society serving nothing but the common good. The most important supporters of this socialist view among literary writers and theorists are Pierre-Joseph Proudhon, Louis Blanc, Émile Augier and François Ponsard. They believe that literary writers can play a pivotal role in the realization of this ideal society because they, more than anyone else, are able to bring about the necessary change of mentality.

Although the ideal of bourgeois writers is not at all unrelated to that of their Romantic contemporaries, the similarities are largely hidden from view by the striking difference in the way in which they value instrumentalization and, as a consequence, modernity as such. Drilled as they were in the Kantian-Romantic concept of instrumentalization as the heteronomous, enslaving force threatening the autonomous experience of the aesthetic, French Romantics declared war on all that smacks of instrumentalization. In a society that is increasingly determined by industrialization, they maintain that literature's power resides precisely in *opposing* itself to society instead of placing itself in its service as the bourgeois writers suggest.

In this respect, French Romantics thus propose a clear change of direction compared to their German predecessors. The latter, too, were critical of industrialization, but they believed that it was not too late for a change *from within*, for a gradual evolution towards a society that would fully meet the poetic principles. About thirty years later, this hope has gone, at least according to the French Romantics. They found themselves at an advanced stage of industrialized society and, what is more, surrounded by an expanded bourgeoisie applauding this industrialization. In addition to this, bourgeois writers were already propagating a gradual evolution from within, a careful cultivation of a pre-given potential. French Romantics, therefore, go on the offensive and aim for an external rather than internal change, their model no longer being that of the playful child, as in the case of their German predecessors, but that of the dandy and the bohemian – unworldly outsiders.

In their polemical debate with bourgeois writers, French Romantics do not miss an opportunity to evoke their most concise slogan: *l'art pour l'art*, art for art's sake. Unfortunately, this slogan has all that is needed to be misunderstood. Not only does it quickly assume a life of its own, but the French Romantics did also far from agree on its actual meaning. This is why one of the first extensive studies on French Romanticism, Cassange's *La théorie de l'art pour l'art chez les derniers romantiques et les premiers réalistes* (1906, *The Theory of Art for Art's Sake in Late Romanticism and Early Realism*), stresses repeatedly that there is not really a school or doctrine of the *l'art pour l'art* movement.[27] The central aim of Cassange's book, therefore, is to unmask the myth of there being some coherent theory about art for art's sake. It is highly doubtful, however, whether he has succeeded, not only given the book's title, but also because this book has been taken as a point of departure by Bourdieu in developing his theory about literature's process of autonomization, which, in turn, was the source of inspiration for anti-autonomist literary histories like that of William Marx.

Whether or not it was misleading, and whether or not Cassange's book played a role in this, in the nineteenth and twentieth century, the slogan of art for art's sake becomes a reality that asks for a clear counter-reaction. Soon, then, it becomes the main target of bourgeois writers, who are as keen on instrumentalism as the Romantics are allergic to it. After all, the bourgeois writer's belief in progress consists of the idea that everybody contributes according to ability to the greater cause of the ideal society. No matter if you are a plumber, an engineer or an artist – everybody must employ their talents and powers for the greater good. Undeniably, the idea of art for art's sake is in straight opposition to that ideal. Bourgeois writers, Cassange observes, 'claimed that art has mission to fulfill other than to stimulate the imagination of layabouts'.[28] If writers are to contribute to a better society, they must do so based on their own talent and, according to the bourgeois writers, the artist's talent is 'to cultivate the sentiments needed for the development of mankind'.[29]

Much as both camps try to be in sharp contrast with each other, the bourgeois allergy for layabouts and the Romantic allergy for instrumentalization spring from the same source: the desire for a harmonious and just society. Like the French Romantics, bourgeois writers want society to be the realization of humanity's full potential, a seamless integration of all parts that would be more than just the sum of these parts. In the end, both 'social' art and art 'for art's sake' serve that goal: 'the opposition between the [social, AvR] literature of the prophets and that of the defenders of the *l'art pour l'art* adage may, in the end, not be as categorical as one believed it to be', Daniel Oster claims in his introduction to Cassange's work: 'Both agree at least on one thing: the artist should again take central stage in society. Priest of art or priest of Humanity, anyhow he is devoted to a holy office.'[30]

The French *l'art pour l'art* debate is the first in a row of very similar polemical debates that take place all over Europe. In Germany, for instance, the *Frühromantiker* are followed by a generation of late Romantics – including Ludwig Tieck, E. T. A. Hoffmann and Joseph Eichendorff – that is confronted with the same advanced industrialization and instrumentalization as their French *confrères*. 'Philistines' is their description of bourgeois writers who ride on the waves of this progress, and the debate between these philistines and the late German Romantics is as fierce as it is on the French side of the French-German border.[31]

In the Netherlands, a similar controversy carried on from 1889 to 1892 in the literary journal *De Nieuwe Gids [The New Journal]*.

The first generation of Dutch Romantics – the so-called 'Eighties Movement' (*Tachtigers*) – find themselves opposed to socialist writers in their view on the best way to shape modern society. Once again, the ambition is nothing less than to 'regauge the artist's task in modern society'.³² Despite their initial mutual sympathies, Romantic writers like Lodewijk Van Deyssel and socialist writers like Frank van der Goes become polar opposites. As is the case in the French *l'art pour l'art* debate, the common ground proves to be more solid, however, than the dust raised by the polemical debate – with hindsight, that is.

It is indeed by looking back that we can see that in these polemical debates, both camps derive their persuasive force, even their *raison d'être*, from their entrenched opposition. This polemic opposition, however, blurs the fact that both camps share the most basic of their premises, which is the very same premise that formed the original scene of modern literature: the idea that literature could and should serve a better society and that the writer should have an eminent role in realization of this goal.³³ The real difference between autonomists and anti-autonomists is therefore not that between art for the sake of art or art for the sake of society, but lies in a disagreement concerning the extent to which (*in casu*: bourgeois) society can fulfil this potential. These debates are therefore not so much *poetic* debates, but ideological debates revolving round the question of the ideal society.³⁴ Consequently, literary debates do not result in a new poetic paradigm after the decline of the Romantic one, but keep on oscillating within the framework set by Romanticism. What is more, for two centuries poetic arguments are a rather unreflective iteration of Romantic arguments, albeit this time not with an eye to an ultimate synthesis, but to continuous opposition.

As it turned out, it is not two types of literature – 'autonomous' versus 'anti-autonomous', 'artistic' versus 'social' and so on – nor 'art' and 'life' that are opposed in these debates, but two types of society. With reference to the famous distinction made by sociologist

Tönnies, we can say that these two types are those of the *community* (*Gemeinschaft*) on the one hand and of *civil society* (*Gesellschaft*) on the other.[35]

As a result of the Industrial Revolution and the rise of the bourgeoisie, *communities* gradually transform into *societies* according to Tönnies, a transformation that he does not necessarily take as degradation. Although one is inclined to conceive of this transformation as a form of disintegration, both types differ mainly in the *way* they unify people: whereas a community is organized around a so-called *Wesenwille*, an intrinsic will of all members to associate themselves, a society is directed by a so-called *Kürwille*, a calculating choice to aim collectively for a certain goal – the employment relation being illustrative of the latter, friendship of the former.

It is safe to say that both forms of collectivity go back to two different ways of conceiving the individual. Not surprisingly then, the clash between the two forms of modernity is instigated by the wish to redefine the human subject after the end of Romanticism. In other words, the two different forms of modernity distinguished above also imply two different forms of individuality. Referring to Georg Simmel in his analysis of the modern subject, Josef Früchtl suggests calling these two forms 'quantitative' and 'qualitative' individualism: 'The first form of individualism emphasizes the ways in which all human beings are equal, the second emphasizes the ways in which all human beings are different. The former focuses on the human being in its universality … the latter on its particularity and uniqueness.'[36]

We can say that early Romanticism – partly inspired by Kant's work and partly critical of it – is the unique historical moment where both forms of individuality coincide. In Romanticism, the individual is indeed encouraged to become a *qualitative* individual, that is autonomous and authentic, but *in doing so*, something like a *quantitative* individuality would be realized: a situation freed from force and oppression where individuals would be alike and equal.

'A fusion of general and particular, in which one shares in the whole at no risk to one's unique specificity', as Terry Eagleton describes this Romantic balancing act.[37] As soon as the temporary entanglement of these two forms of individuality is disentangled, quantitative and qualitative individuality re-emerge as opposite forms and serve again as the ideals of respectively 'society' and 'community' central to the post-Romantic debates about literary autonomy.

A new status quo

Again, it is Rancière who has given one of the most tersely formulated analyses of this Janus-faced modernity. Modernity, or rather the *notion* of modernity, has an important shortcoming, Rancière observes in *The Politics of Aesthetics: Distribution of the Sensible* (2004).[38] That is, the notion of 'modernity' leads one to suspect the existence of one coherent theoretical framework that we could call 'modernity'. The opposite is true, Rancière maintains: 'the notion of modernity ... seems to have been deliberately invented to prevent a clear understanding of the transformations of art and its relationships with the other species of collective experience.'[39] The suggestion of a coherent theoretical framework evoked by the notion of modernity has in other words *blocked* our view on the real dynamics of modernity, dynamics that have not only produced abstract art, but also the arts-and-craft movement, not only Mallarmé, but also Sartre.

When one takes a closer look at the post-Romantic aesthetic debates, one should indeed conclude that modernity presents itself in *two different forms*, two forms that revert back to the original Romantic conjunction: 'Both of them, without analyzing it, rely on the contradiction constitutive of the aesthetic regime of the arts, which ... sets down, at one and the same time, the autonomy of art and its identification with a moment in life's process of self-formation.'[40]

What Rancière had indicated as the 'emplotment of autonomy and heteronomy' in his essay on Schiller is here referred to as the contradiction constitutive of the aesthetic regime. The presumably homogeneous period of modernity is actually a schizophrenic reality that is rooted in the two-sided ground of early German Romanticism. The notion of modernity is but the patch that conceals the fundamental abyss between the two sides.

Importantly, these two forms of modernity – which I call autonomism and anti-autonomism – *together* make up post-Romantic aesthetic modernity, like two sides of the same picture. That is to say that *both* sides are in a way a continuation of the Romantic project that marked the birth of modern literature. This view can be taken as a severe criticism of literary histories like that by William Marx that present modernity as a univocal process of autonomization and thereby reduce it to the autonomist side of the picture. Not only is modernity less univocal than these theories suggest, but it is not a process of autonomization either – or only when this process is paired with an equally dominant process of anti-autonomization.

Rancière's clearest illustration of the two-sidedness of post-Romantic modernity is the example of Russian Futurism which, in addition to being a revolutionary movement, also aimed at a radical renewal of the literary form. In stressing this two-sidedness, however, Rancière did not explain *why* post-Romantic dynamics resulted in the simultaneous isolation of these two sides, as is the aim of this chapter. As I have tried to show, these dynamics are not so much the *internal* dynamics of particular literary movements like Futurism but, first and foremost, the dynamics *between* the literary movements that emerged after the decline of the Romantic paradigm. It is only in polemic debate with bourgeois writers, that French Romantics like Victor Cousin and Théophile Gautier insisted on the principle of *l'art pour l'art*. As it is in polemic debate with Surrealism that Sartre developed his ideas of literary commitment, as it is in reaction to popular art and kitsch that Adorno stepped into the breach for artistic autonomy, and as it is in reaction to historicist approaches that the New Critics defended the self-referential text.

Characterizing post-Romantic modernity as a battle between two opposite and incompatible sides, as I just did, might be a necessary adjustment to the one-sided determinist literary histories that tend only to highlight literature's autonomization; it is also somewhat misleading. In recent decades, these antagonistic dynamics have actually to a high degree calmed down within the domain of literary studies. Despite the ongoing oscillation between the key parameters of Romantics – art and life, autonomy and heteronomy, individual and society, and so on – literary studies seem to have found a new and relatively solid, dualistic, theoretical basis, a new status quo. This theoretical basis does not so much rely on the ideological distinction between two forms of modernity, but on the more pragmatic one between the literary *text* and its *context*. The polemical opposition between autonomism and anti-autonomism has thus been gradually transformed into that between text and context respectively.

A clear example of this transformation can once again be found in M. H. Abrams's *The Mirror and the Lamp*, which has not only been influential because of its theory of Romanticism, but also because it offered the more scientific approach to literature applauded in twentieth-century literary studies.[41] In his study, Abrams proposes to map the field of literary criticism and makes an influential case for the existence of four 'co-ordinates of art criticism' that can help to dissect the research object of literary criticism: the 'artist', the 'work', the 'audience' and the 'universe'.[42] According to Abrams, these four coordinates imply four kinds of literary theory that all take one of these coordinates as their main focus: respectively the expressive, objective, pragmatic and mimetic theories.

It is not the schematic fourfold itself that is significant, since it echoes many other literary (meta-)theories, but Abrams's *interpretation* of these four coordinates. This interpretation is primarily a historical one: whereas the pragmatic and mimetic theories were dominant before Romanticism, Romanticism itself marks the emergence of the expressive theory according to Abrams. This is the shift from the mirror to the lamp. Although Abrams wants to limit himself to a description of this historical shift, he does suggest that *after* Romanticism, a fourth type of literary theory emerged – the objective one – that is in his view exemplified by the New Criticism of many of his contemporaries.

It is this historical presentation of the fourfold that subsequently receives a more systematic interpretation in Abrams's work, because of a suggested *dichotomy* between the pragmatic, mimetic and expressive literary theories on the one hand, and the objective one on the other hand. This dichotomy remains somewhat implicit, but is nevertheless clearly shaping Abrams's view. The most concise formulation of this dichotomy can be found in the entry Abrams composed himself in *The New Princeton Encyclopedia of Poetry and Poetics*:

> Commonly a critic takes one of these elements or relations [universe, artist, audience, or work, AvR] as cardinal and refers the poem either to the external world or to the audience or to the poet as preponderantly 'the source, and end, and test of art'; *or alternatively*, she or he considers the poem as a self-sufficient entity best analyzed in theoretical isolation. ... These varied orientations give us, in a preliminary way, four broad types of poetic theory, which may be labeled mimetic, pragmatic, expressive, and objective.[43]

Upon closer consideration, Abrams's influential overview of Western literary theories appears, therefore, to superimpose a dualistic model on the quadrilateral one. The result is a conceptualization of all four coordinates, as well as their interrelations, in terms of a prior conceptualization of the *text* in relation to its *context*. It is only at a later stage that the work's context is specified as being chiefly related to the author ('artist'), the reader ('audience'), or to reality ('universe'). Whereas objective theories focus *solely* on the literary text, as Abrams states, in expressive, pragmatic, and mimetic theories attention is *also* paid to anti-autonomist aspects such as the cultural or autobiographical background of the author, the alleged effects of literary works on readers, or topical events in everyday reality.

In other words: compared to the last three, which *do* pay attention to the 'whole situation of art', the objective literary theory that emerged with twentieth-century New Criticism is, according to Abrams, fundamentally different because it considers the literary work 'in theoretical isolation' from these external factors. This view, however, ensues from a forced interpretation of the fourfold system of literary coordinates that, for its part, follows the standard model of communication in terms of sender-message-receiver. Transposing the standard model of communication into the domain of literature, however, is a remarkable choice since Romanticism has significantly changed the view of literature as a form of communication.

In this chapter, I have described this change as the hermeneutic turn, which implies that literature is no longer expressing a truth external to it, but its *proper* truth. This is not a shift from a communicative form of literature to a non-communicative one, but a shift in the way communication itself is understood. From Romanticism onwards, the literary work is not conceived as isolated from its surroundings, but starting to engage differently with these surroundings. Abrams's conclusion, therefore, that twentieth-century literary theory presents the literary work as isolated from the external world is the result of a forced attempt to conceive of post-Romantic literary theory in terms of a pre-Romantic view on communication. Nevertheless, it is precisely this interpretation of the literary text as isolated from its context that became widespread.

Institutional separation

I have claimed above that modernity's polemical debates, like the French *l'art pour l'art* debate, were not so much poetical, but rather sociopolitical debates. By translating them in terms of text and context, however, these sociopolitical debates are as it were remodelled, after the fact, into poetical ones – which disguises their sociopolitical nature even further.

The result is, as stated, a fundamental dichotomy between theories dealing with literature-as-text and theories dealing with literature-in-context. 'Literature', in this case, is no longer a description of a specific way of engaging with reality, but of an isolated textual object that may or may not be considered in relation to its context. Dependent on the type of literature, its value, as it is now believed, lies either in the work itself or is external to it. Or in Abrams's vocabulary, its value is either 'intrinsic' or 'extrinsic'. Having indicated that since the literature of Romanticism has become unrelated to the categories of truth and untruth, Abrams continues:

> Let us divide theories of poetic value into two broadly distinguishable classes:
> 1. Poetry has intrinsic value, and as poetry, only intrinsic value. It is to be estimated by the literary critic solely as poetry, and as an end in itself, without reference to its possible effects on thought, feeling or the conduct of its readers.
> 2. Poetry has intrinsic value, *but also* extrinsic value, as a means to moral and social effects beyond itself. The two cannot (or at least, should not) be separated by the critic in estimating its poetic worth.[44]

Once again, the distinction between these two classes is not only presented as a distinction between literature-as-text and literature-in-context, but the former class is also presented as a reduced version of the second. Compared to the mimetic, pragmatic and expressive literary theories that *also* pay attention to literature's external effects, contemporary post-Romantic theory according to Abrams chooses not to account for these effects, because it isolates the work from its context. Not surprisingly then, Abrams's objective literary theory has become generally known as the theory of *autonomism*.

Although Abrams clearly wants to distinguish this objective theory from the Romantic-expressive one, the roots of the former are usually placed within Romanticism. Retrospectively, the idea of the autonomous, isolated literary text is thus attributed to the paradigm shift that took place with Romanticism and that Abrams described in terms of a shift from the mirror to the lamp.

According to Jonathan Loesberg, it is the English Romantic poet Coleridge who played a pivotal role in this retrospective conception of the Romantic paradigm. Although Coleridge himself emphasized his indebtedness to the tradition of Kant and the early German Romantics, he gave a rather significant twist to this tradition. Coleridge took the notion of 'organic unity' – a notion closely related to that of the undivided – and made a distinction between two different types of organicism: an internal and an external one. According to Coleridge, the *internal* organic unity refers to the Romantic idea of the undivided, while the *external* unity stands for the atomized and mechanized civil society that was under attack within this Romantic idea. However, although the Romantic paradigm indeed opposed itself to this atomized form of society, a differentiation between an internal and an external form of unity is diametrically opposed to the Romantic paradigm, if not to say to the very idea of an organic unity. Within the Romantic paradigm, organicism implies nothing other than the *integration* of the internal and the external into one undivided organism. 'Coleridge's claim of two forms of organization, external mechanism and internal and integral organicism, is', as is maintained by Loesberg, therefore 'in terms of his German idealist sources, simply incoherent.'[45] Nevertheless, it is this very idea of an *isolated internal coherence* that has been taken by Coleridge as the core of Romantic aesthetics – an interpretation that underlies the widespread concept of the artwork as an isolated, self-referential unity that is, for instance, defended by the New Critics.[46]

It is on the basis of this retrospective interpretation of the Romantic paradigm that the notion of autonomy was able to adopt the remarkable meaning it has today and that the distinction between autonomism and anti-autonomism could coincide with the distinction between text-oriented and context-oriented approaches to literature. 'Autonomy' is no longer regarded as an overall aesthetic stance or judgement, as the Romantics maintained, but is reduced to, or even identified with, the sole aspect of the literary practice that can best be opposed to 'heteronomy-focused' approaches: the isolated text. This reduction has been so radical that notions such as 'autonomy' and 'autonomism' are now automatically associated with a text-oriented approach to literature, whereas anti-autonomism, conversely, is identified with the focus on contextual factors.[47]

Because of this categorical distinction between text-oriented and context-oriented approaches, a very clear division of labour enters the institutional framework of literary studies. Whereas the Romantic paradigm conceived of literature as an all-encompassing phenomenon that was therefore also to be investigated from all sides, the field of literary studies gradually divides itself into all kinds of sub-disciplines – text analysis, reader response theory, sociological, institutional, historical and biographical approaches, and so on – that all have their proper methodology, corpus and research agenda. Not only is this division of labour very well-organized, it also explains why post-Romantic debates gradually appeased into a new, seemingly stable status quo.

Beneath the calm surface of this new status quo, however, the tension is increasing. Although meticulously arranged, the division between text-oriented approaches and context-oriented approaches remains the implicit source of all kinds of conceptual difficulties, especially when it comes to making sense of the functioning of literature within the world. As a matter of fact, most literary research of the past decades, especially in New Historicism, postcolonial literary studies and gender studies, is motivated by research questions that aim to overcome the gap between text and context.[48]

Similarly, the more recent studies on literary autonomy also try to connect text and context. In *Fictions of Autonomy* (2003), Andrew Goldstone, for instance, claims: 'My overarching thesis: the pursuit of autonomy leads modernist writers to take account of, and seek to transform, the social relations of their literary production.'[49] A comparable approach can be found in Gregory Jusdanis's *Fiction Agonistes* (2010): 'I hope to reconcile two antithetical approaches: that art is an autonomous entity and that it is social convention.'[50] Finally, in his *Satirizing Modernism: Autonomy, Romanticism, and the Avant-Garde* (2017), Emmett Stinson, too, hopes 'to move beyond the binary in which aesthetic autonomy is viewed as either as [*sic*] an elitist escape from reality or as a model for enacting utopian social change', by considering 'how the notion of autonomy in avant-garde satires is intimately linked to a set of social contexts that cannot be separated from the generic history of satire as form.'[51]

Although it is interesting to see how these attempts can reveal the complexity of literature as an object of research, I have tried to show in this chapter that the two antithetical positions that they want to reconcile are the result of the lack of an overarching theoretical framework. The solution to this is, in my view, not a reconciliation of both sides, but the articulation of a new paradigmatic framework in which the two sides do not even appear as two sides to begin with. Two centuries after Romanticism, therefore, we do not need to defend or attack the notion of literary autonomy, but we have to reconsider, from a contemporary perspective, the Romantic aspiration that underlies the concept of modern literature.

The dual heritage of Romanticism

Just like the Enlightenment ideas of subjectivity and truth, the Romantic paradigm is not rejected in one go within modernity, but is gradually refined, criticized and questioned. Even what is usually called 'post-modernity' is not so much a clean break with modernity, but rather one of the phases in this process of critical refinement.[52] Although the incredulity towards modernity's grand narratives is one of the most important shifts in twentieth-century intellectual history, this incredulity is not a farewell to the intellectual project of modernity; it merely lays bare this project in a more ruthless manner.

With hindsight, it can be argued that the refinement, critique and questioning of the Romantic paradigm was inspired by a growing awareness of what we are inclined to call today the contingent *situatedness* of the subject and its cultural products – an awareness that was also that of the Romantics, but that was developed more substantially after Romanticism. In times like ours, where existentialism and Darwinism have permeated society, where the idea of embodied cognition is one of the basic psychological premises, and where even the most widely shared values are considered to be context-related, it is difficult to understand that the idea of situatedness itself has a history. Nevertheless, it is clear that the early-nineteenth-century mindset was such that this idea of situatedness could only arise in an *indirect* way, that is, *via the idea of heteronomy* or, indeed, as Rancière rightly observed, via a complex mutual entanglement of autonomy and heteronomy. Kant's influential opposition between these two terms has turned every attempt to unite them into an attempt to bridge them *afterwards*. The unchallenged point of departure was the supposed *opposition* between autonomy and heteronomy, a point of departure that has thus significantly obstructed the opportunity for a new paradigm to emerge. After all, from this dualistic point of departure, something like an intrinsic connection between autonomy and heteronomy is simply *unconceivable*.

For more than a century, then, Western thought about the situatedness of the subject and its cultural products has been sidetracked. This is also the conclusion Alberto Toscano draws in his *The Theatre of Production: Philosophy and Individuation between Kant and Deleuze* (2006). According to Toscano, a break of the deadlock of Kantian dualism could only be found in a view on the subject that he somewhat misleadingly calls 'organic'. Neither Kant, nor his Romantic followers have succeeded in conceiving the organic unity of the subject with its environment, despite the abundant organic metaphors used by the latter: 'The inability truly to incorporate the problem of the organic either within the Critical system [of Kant, AvR] itself or as a component in a new problematic … will be exhibited as the negative site of a new philosophical intervention.'[53] This inability has, in other words, been philosophy's driving force for quite some time. Like a fly banging against a window attempting freedom, Western thought has in vain tried to find an escape from dualism. As Rudolphe Gasché rightly states in his *Of Minimal Things: Studies on the Notion of Relation* (1999), it is only during the twentieth century that we are able to conceive of 'connection' or 'relation' on such a fundamental level that we are able to surmount the Kantian dualism between autonomy and heteronomy.[54]

The next chapter will show that the solution to this dualism lies in an *ontological approach* to this relationality. Enabling literature to be conceived of as fundamentally situated, demands in other words a new perspective on the way literature *is*, that is, on its *mode of existence*. Key to this perspective is locating the connection between art and life, the artistic and the social, the autonomous and the heteronomous already on the level of literature's mode of existence, that is, *prior to* the emergence of these oppositions, and even prior to the content or effects of literary works. Instead of situating the heritage of Romanticism on either of the two sides of modernity, it should be reconsidered in its entirety within a new paradigm.

3

The Relational Paradigm

From antagonism to relationality

Paradigm shifts tend to hide themselves from view. They take place offstage, in an intermediary zone, an intermediary time. And it is only when perceiving the new stage that one realizes that it must have been there already for quite some time. In this last chapter, I will try to conceptualize the replacements and transformations that have been hidden from view. As stated earlier, the transition to the relational paradigm had already started in late-twentieth- and twenty-first-century philosophy and disciplines inspired by philosophy. I will take these philosophical developments as a starting point in sketching a relational paradigm for the study of literature. In the previous chapter, I have described this task as the construction of a new magnetic field, enabling the antagonistic dynamics between autonomist and anti-autonomist positions to be overcome.

Before commencing the conceptualization of the relational paradigm, however, we may wonder whether overcoming the antagonistic dynamics is a desirable option to begin with. Is literature's power not dependent on this very antagonism? This is a claim that has often been defended during the past few centuries. Its two most fervent representatives are undoubtedly Adorno and Rancière who, at least to some extent, try not to choose sides in the debate between autonomism and anti-autonomism, but instead attempt *constructively to preserve* the opposition between the two. Literature's truth according to them is not on either of the two sides, but can be found in the antagonistic dynamics themselves. 'The division itself is the truth', as Adorno has it.[1]

In contemporary scholarship, this plea for a constructive opposition is widely shared. In his *Fiction Agonistes* (2010), Jusdanis, for instance, closely follows Adorno in his aim 'to reconcile two antithetical approaches: that art is an autonomous entity and that it is a social convention'.[2] On the one hand, literature is presented as an inextricable part of reality; an empirical fact, a human product that is part and parcel of a social and historical reality. On the other hand, it is deemed characteristic of literature to disengage from that reality by refusing to obey its laws. Authentic or successful literature is thus both at the heart of social reality and opposed to it – a very rare position that only very few authors, among whom are Kafka and Beckett, were able to hold according to Adorno. However rare it may be, according to many a scholar it is this very position of internal outsider or external insider that allows literature to have the critical potential that makes it a socially relevant practice, a counter-voice that is social precisely *because* it is a counter-voice.[3]

In a similar vein, Rancière, whose work has become increasingly popular the past few decades, is looking for a productive form of antagonism. Key to what he calls the contemporary aesthetic regime is, as stated, the 'emplotment' of autonomy and heteronomy. Within the aesthetic regime, Rancière maintains, art is autonomous because it no longer needs to copy the established sociopolitical structures. Paradoxically, however, *because* of that, art is also social according to Rancière. More precisely, artistic freedom suppresses the distinction between art and life, since everything can be turned into a work of art. 'Art exists as a *separate* world since *everything* can belong to it',[4] is how Rancière formulates this paradox in *Aisthesis* (2013).

This paradoxical situation embodies in Rancière's view a productive tension between autonomy and anti-autonomy that enables literature to interrupt and rearrange certain social structures. After all, since literature is exempt from copying these social structures, it can shed light on that which is excluded from or hidden by them, Rancière maintains. His favourite illustration of this principle are the works of Flaubert and Balzac. At a time when describing people and subjects of moral standing was still the norm, both Flaubert and Balzac shifted their attention to pitiful creatures like the adulteress Emma Bovary and to ordinary life's most trivial of subjects. By breaking the norm, the literary works of Flaubert and Balzac evoked a *redistribution* of the dominant social order, a redistribution that in the end led to an overall refutation of hierarchical categories.[5] In doing so, literature, Rancière would say, creates a new form of visibility *within* the existing one.[6]

Whereas Adorno's writer is clearly an outsider, albeit situated within society, Rancière's writer is itself creating some sort of new inside–outside relationship. Both Rancière and Adorno, however, stress that it is literature's autonomy that enables it to be critical of society. Behind the opposition between autonomy and heteronomy that Rancière and Adorno wish to preserve for the sake of this critical potential is an emancipatory project that starts from the assumption that every society is based on some form of oppression that is consciously or unconsciously concealed in the way it presents itself. Only an uncommon form of representation can reveal what is concealed, which is why art, according to Rancière, 'does not make visible; it imposes presence'.[7]

Although theories like Rancière's and Adorno's have greatly helped to regain the complexity and versatility of the notions of literary autonomy and social commitment, their scope, in the end, is limited. The reason is that these emancipatory analyses are still rooted within the nineteenth-century Romantic conceptual framework that *opposes* autonomy and heteronomy.[8] Theories such as Adorno's and Rancière's indeed do not appease the post-Romantic antagonism, but instead fan its fire. Despite their attempt to take the antagonism *itself* as their point of departure and to make it productive, their theories are, without much ado, generally situated on the autonomist side – and probably rightly so. After all, the ultimate goal of aesthetic theories such as these is to emancipate the subject from suppressing social structures. Albeit in its most suspicious manifestation, Adorno and Rancière are still holding on to the very promise of the Enlightenment: that of the autonomous subject.[9]

It is therefore about time we searched elsewhere for the solution to modernity's theoretical impasse: not in literature's emancipatory criticism, but in an *ontological* approach to literature. As stated, I propose calling this approach 'relational'. This relational paradigm does not take as its starting point the opposition of autonomy and heteronomy – an opposition that is inextricably bound to the eighteenth-century mindset from which it emerged – but starts from the *underlying aspiration* of Romantic aesthetics to overcome this opposition. It does not therefore so much propose a completely different view on modern literature as a reinterpretation, following recent developments in philosophy, of the aspiration that formed its inalienable foundation. An attempt, in other words, to *re-gauge*, from a contemporary perspective, what is and has always been at stake in modern literature: the aspiration to overcome or entangle the opposition of autonomy and heteronomy, art and society.

The forgetfulness of literature

I am not the first one to propose a concept of modern literature as relational. Twentieth-century movements such as George Dickie's and Arthur Danto's institutionalism or Pierre Bourdieu's sociology of art were already characterized as something of a sociological 'relational turn' in the study of art.[10] Central to this sociological turn is the view that 'art' or 'literature' are open concepts that are not determined by intrinsic qualities of the artistic object, but rather by the way they function amidst a web of relations and institutions that Danto simply calls 'the artworld'.[11]

Other movements that are sometimes called 'relational' are that of New Historicism or, more broadly, Cultural Studies, which, since its international breakthrough in the 1980s, has become one of the most dominant approaches within the field of literary studies. These movements pay close attention to the sociocultural, political or historical constructions that fundamentally determine the production, reception and meaning of the literary work. Here, the presumed relationality of literature is less an institutional or sociological one and more of an ideological one.[12] In a way, these sociological and ideological approaches come down to an increasing emphasis on what Seigel, in his study on *The Idea of the Self*, calls the 'relational dimension' of selfhood, that is, the perspective on selfhood in which 'ourselves are what our relations with society and with others shape or allow us to be'.[13]

The relational paradigm I propose in this last chapter, however, differs from the above-mentioned views. Instead of conceiving of literature's relationality on the institutional or sociocultural level, I suggest it should be understood on the *ontological* level. The difference between these two levels reverts to Heidegger's influential distinction between the ontic and the ontological.

The *ontic* level is that of things, *beings*. These are the table at which I am sitting, the book I am reading, I myself. In brief, the ontic level concerns everything that exists and that can be described in terms of its specific characteristics and possibly in its interconnection with other things that exist. In the case of literature, these characteristics may, for instance, be the style and theme of a literary work, the way it has been received or its institutional context. *Ontologically* speaking, though, nothing has been said yet about literature when describing these ontic characteristics. On the ontological level, it is the *mode of being* of these beings that is at stake, *the way they exist*. This mode of being is not one of the characteristics of the thing, of literature in this case. It is rather the way in which that thing presents itself to us, even before we are inclined to ascribe certain characteristics that we may or may not investigate in their interconnectedness.

The ontological level, in other words, *precedes* the ontic level. Questions regarding this ontological level are not: what are the characteristics of this literary work? What are its possible interpretations? In what way does it relate to the current socio-political reality? It is rather questions such as: what kind of thing is literature? How can something like literature exist? Does a literary work exist in the same way as other types of work? In what way does literature affect the way I am experiencing my own mode of being? Difficulties arise, of course, when one wants to describe the ontological level of literature *as such*, that is, without touching on the textual characteristics or the sociocultural context of specific literary works. After all, when dealing with literature we are always dealing with specific ontic characteristics of a work: its style, author, referential meaning, tradition and so on. Questioning in what way a literary work exists is therefore never unrelated to an analysis of these characteristics. The point is, however, that we should avoid *conflating* an analysis of the latter – that is, of the characteristics of such and such literary entity – with the more fundamental analysis of the way in which literature as such presents itself – that is, with an analysis of the mode of *being* of literary entities.

The reason why we need such an ontological approach to literature is as simple as it is far-reaching. Since the decline of the Romantic paradigm, we suffer from what I propose calling a *forgetfulness of literature*, which is basically a forgetfulness of the question of literature's mode of being. As Heidegger had it, modern human beings suffer from what he calls a 'forgetfulness of being', because they have become completely oblivious to the being of beings, that is to the way things *are*, in their fervent attempts to classify and categorize these things. In defining, classifying and mapping all things surrounding them, modern human beings have completely forgotten to dwell upon the marvellous fact that these things *exist* to begin with, and to wonder how on earth this is possible. Similarly, I would argue, we have gradually forgotten about truly considering the marvellous fact that something like literature exists and the exceptional mode of being that literature is. Instead of asking ourselves what this mode of being consists of, we have lost ourselves in polemic debates about literature's presumed characteristics: autonomous or social, elitist or popular, aesthetic or ethical, or a combination of all these. However, irrespective of these characteristics, or rather *through* them or *implied by* them, the mere fact that it is a work of *literature* is utterly significant for the way in which it is, that is, for the way it exists in the world. A paradigm able to explain the way literature functions in current society, therefore, has to depart from the question as to what literature's way of being is.

Obviously, within the relational paradigm, the answer to that question is different to what it was in the Romantic paradigm. Whereas the Romantic paradigm explained the particular mode of being of literature in terms of its individuality, as something *undivided*, a (future) whole, the relational paradigm explains literature's particular mode of being in terms of its relationality. As has been stated, this ontological relationality is different from an ontic form of relationality. Ontologically speaking, literature's relationality does not concern the sociocultural or institutional web of relations of which literary works are a part, as the sociology of literature or Cultural Studies have it. Saying that literature is relational on an ontological level means saying that literature's mode of being – irrespective of its textual, cultural or institutional qualities albeit through them – is relational: literature *is* always in the mode of a relation, *is* nothing but a relation, even when it tries to sever all ties with everyday reality. Put differently:

ontologically speaking there is no world to which literature is, or is not, connected, but literature itself is a way of relating to the world.[14]

Whereas ontic approaches to literature's relationality ultimately come down to a form of contextualism and, in doing so, subscribe to the problematic dualist framework of modernity that opposes a 'text' and a 'context' that are subsequently explained in terms of their interaction and connectedness, an ontological approach to its relationality invalidates this concept of literature as a work within a specific context. Because of its relational mode of existence, literature is primarily a relational happening, an act, rather than an established work: it is a form of *being* in the world, rather than a *thing* in the world.[15]

One of the first to focus on this ontological relationality in the domain of aesthetics was Nicolas Bourriaud. In his *Relational Aesthetics* (2002), Bourriaud – at that time curator of the Palais de Tokyo – tried to conceptualize the art practice of participatory art in the 1980s and 1990s. How to conceive, for instance, the artwork of Rirkit Tiravanja, who installed a picnic table and cooking devices in the museum hall, inviting visitors to have a seat and share some soup (*pad thai*, 1990), or Alix Lambert's *Wedding Piece* (1992), in which she subsequently gets married to, and divorced from, three men and a woman. Or, lastly, *Turkish Jokes* (1994) by Jens Haaning, consisting of the transmission of Turkish-spoken jokes through speakers located at one of Copenhagen's public squares, thereby temporarily creating a small society of insiders?

One could conceive of these works of participation art as somewhat easy forms of social or political activism, as Rancière does in his criticism of Bourriaud.[16] For Bourriaud, however, this is not what is at stake. According to Bourriaud, it is mainly the encounter itself that is key to these works, the engagement with each other in the creation and experience of some form of community – not as a prefiguration of a utopian community or as part of a political programme, but in its most basic and real form, here and now. These artworks express for Bourriaud what Althusser had called the 'materialism of the encounter' or 'aleatory materialism'; a random encounter that consists of a minimal displacement that nevertheless can produce a whole new series of encounters.[17]

Rancière's critical reaction is part of a much broader sceptical reception of Bourriaud's *Relational Aesthetics*. With hindsight, the heated discussion accompanying its publication seems to be due to the attempt to fit Bourriaud's relational theory into the antagonistic grid of the two opposed forms of modernity. The artists described by Bourriaud should then be considered 'social artists', but of the outdated kind. In his answer to Rancière's accusations, Bourriaud himself makes a similar observation:

> It seems that the debates that have been raised by the 'relational' in art since the publication of the book essentially revolve around the respective positions of ethics, the political and aesthetics in the artistic practices that are described. These practices have been suspected of putting morals above form, generating a purely 'social' or even 'Christian' or 'compassionate' art; they have been accused of proposing an angelic ethical model, masking the existing conflicts in society.[18]

What is highlighted by Bourriaud's analysis, however, is that these artists aimed precisely at *countering* modernity's antagonism by plainly showing the mode of existence of their artworks. According to Bourriaud, participation art does not so much raise the question as to what socially committed art is, but rather the more basic question as to what art is.

The answer to *that* question – not to that of the politics or ethics of art – lies in its relationality. According to Bourriaud, this kind of participatory artwork is a matter of a relational encounter rather than of a closed-off form: 'In observing contemporary artistic practices, we ought to talk of "formations" rather than "forms". Unlike an object that is closed in on itself by the intervention of a style and a signature, present-day art shows that form only exists in the encounter'.[19] The key to participation art, in other words, is no longer the intention of the artist, nor the work's identifiable form, but the work's 'formation', that is the dynamic relationship between the more or less contingent elements of the objects, the participants, the space and time that bring the work into existence.

As a result, it is not *as* art that these kinds of works present themselves in the public sphere – or, perhaps, fail to do so – but it is rather the formation of that public sphere itself that turns them into artworks. This can be considered a frontal attack on the poetic scheme that has been described by Abrams and that has been so influential for modernity's dualism. In terms of Abrams's scheme for the artwork, the artist, the audience and the universe, the poetics concerning participation art can hardly be identified with one of the coordinates, but should rather be understood as dealing with a specific temporal synthesis of all of them. The ontological status of his temporal synthesis is, by definition, precarious. These works disappear as easily as they emerge and are, according to Bourriaud, for this very reason exemplary expressions of our present mode of existence, in which identities have become fluid as a result of globalization and multiculturalism and are dependent on multiple and often temporary networks.[20]

Literature as a way of being in the world

Bourriaud's relational aesthetics is restricted to a very specific form of art – participatory art – and is, as stated, generally received as a specific view on the political dimension of modern art. The potential scope of this relational aesthetics, however, is much broader, because it invites us to interpret the relationality of art, including literature, not merely on a societal level, but more fundamentally, on an ontological one.[21]

If Bourriaud's relational aesthetics is part of a philosophical tradition, it is therefore not that of social or political philosophy, but that of the ontologies of art developed by twentieth-century post-structuralist thinkers such as Blanchot, Lyotard, Derrida and Nancy. In these ontologies of art, art is firstly considered to be an *event* rather than an artefact, a unique temporal and local happening which, for that very reason, defies attempts to define it. It is this kind of twentieth-century aesthetics of the event that Bourriaud translates in terms of the relational and that informs the relational paradigm developed in this chapter.

To develop the broad outlines of this relational paradigm further, I shall take my cue from the work of Jean-Luc Nancy. By reconsidering the ontological conditions of several facets of our community – globalization, arts, technology, religion – Nancy reverts to Heidegger's existential ontology, reinterpreted from a post-structuralist perspective, rather than to the heritage of Kant. Although literature is but one of the domains addressed by Nancy, his work offers quite a clear lead for developing a relational view on literature's ontology.[22] As has been said, key to this view is the invitation to conceive of literature not as an object, but as a way of being; a way of being, moreover, that, according to Nancy, is not opposed to the world or distanced from it, but *in* the world.

Following Nancy, the first step to be taken in considering literature as a form of being in the world rather than as opposed to it, is to change our conception fundamentally of the *world* itself. Whereas eighteenth and nineteenth-century philosophers such as Kant were inclined to speak of 'the' world as if it were some homogenous entity, Nancy believes it to be a mistake to think in terms of *a* world, of *the* world as distinct from an unworldly realm or, for that matter, of possible worlds. Ultimately, the present-day interpretation of literary autonomy as a retreat from the world is still supported by this eighteenth and nineteenth-century view of the world.

According to Nancy, however, neither the world, nor being are fixed entities. There is no such thing as *the* world. Since 'we' and 'world' co-emerge and constitute each other, Nancy maintains, there are only virtually consistent wholes of people, things, ideas and so on that make sense and in which we live and by which we live. These are all worlds, or again and again *a* world. Only when we take 'world' in this sense, can we conceive of relationality – including literature's relationality – on an ontological level, Nancy argues.[23] Since being in 'the' world is always, and always anew, a relational mode of being, it is, at any moment, a matter of *coexistence*. This means that being in the world is always both singular – here and now in this specific world – and plural – a mode of being with the whole of people, things, ideas and so on that together constitute this world.

Now that we have redefined what 'world', and consequently a relational being in the world, means, we can catch a glimpse of what it means to conceive of literature as a relational mode of being in the world. Literature, Nancy maintains here, is a 'living relation'.[24] It is, in other words, a form of renewing and relating (the French *relater* means both 'to tell' and 'to relate') 'world', a world that is nothing but this renewed relating, time and again. But what is this living relation in the case of literature? Here, Nancy reverts to a seemingly traditional poetic idea: that of the *symbol*. Literary works, Nancy argues, are relational because they are symbolic. It is important to note here that Nancy interprets the symbolic in the original sense of the word *sumbolon*, combining or joining, thereby referring to the ancient Greek practice of matching the two pieces of a broken piece of pottery to identify friends. 'The proper value of symbolism', he argues, 'is in making a *symbol*, that is, in making a connection or a joining, and in giving a face to this liaison by making an *image*'.[25]

Instead of an abstract relationship that can be generalized, the symbolic is for Nancy the singular incarnation of relationality. In describing literature as symbolic, Nancy thus clearly distinguishes himself from the aesthetic paradigm opened up by Kant, in which the symbolic was conceived of as the sensible presentation of some general idea (i.e. a beautiful form as a symbol of morality). According to Nancy, symbolization is thus not a form of *representing*, but is itself a form of *relating*, as are the jokes transmitted on the Copenhagen square in the participatory artwork of Jens Haaning, or the weddings solemnized in Alix Lambert's *Wedding Pieces*. In the case of a literary work, too, we may maintain that insofar as it is presenting something, it is first and foremost the presentation of the act of relating itself. Or as Nancy has it: 'the symbolic is what is real in such a relation.'[26] A novel is, in the act of reading or writing it, bringing forth a mode of being in the world that is constituted by the peculiarities of the novel's plot, its turns of phrase and associations with other books that have been read, together with random environmental factors like grief over a lost lover, the intrusive sound of a dog barking or the bleak light seeping through the curtains.

Following Nancy, we could say that the category of the relational defines the poetic as an exemplary manifestation of the *relationality* of our being, similarly to the way in which the Romantic category of the individual defined the poetic as an exemplary manifestation of the assumed *individuality* of our being. Apart from being a shift from individuality to relationality, this shift from the Romantic to the relational paradigm can be conceived of as a shift from the absolute to the contingent. But how come? Why did individuality as the prime category give way to that of relationality? And in what sense are the aspirations of the Romantic paradigm re-gauged within the relational paradigm, as I stated above?

Ever since the collapse of the Romantic paradigm, the remnants of this paradigm have been shifted back and forth between autonomists and anti-autonomists for want of a new all-encompassing paradigm. Usually, it is a widely shared sense of unease that forms the very first impetus to such a new paradigm. In the case of the Romantic one, this unease is felt in Novalis's famous call that 'we need to romanticize the world', adding: 'This yields again its original meaning. Romanticising is nothing else than a qualitative potentisation. In this operation, the lower self becomes identified with a better self.'[27] The essence of the Romantic paradigm is summarized in these words. The original meaning of the world has disappeared and will only be regained by means of a poetic potential that will firstly be employed by the individual person and that will subsequently stretch to the interrelated level of the collective individual, that is, of society.

The impetus leading to the relational paradigm is both very similar and radically different from that of Novalis's unease. Two centuries after Novalis's call, Nancy says in *The Inoperative Community* (1991):

> What 'there is' in place of communication is neither the subject nor communal being, but community and sharing. ... Perhaps, in truth, there is nothing to say. Perhaps we should not seek a word or a concept for it, but rather recognize in the thought of community a theoretical excess (or more precisely, an excess in relation to the theoretical) that would oblige us to adopt *another praxis of discourse and community* ... something that would be the sharing of community in and by its writing, *its literature*.[28]

In our times, as in Novalis's times, we have lost the sense of what our community is all about, Nancy maintains. And in our times, as in Novalis's times, he continues, the way of regaining this sense seems to lie in the way literature expresses our community. These two eras differ, however, in their view of *what* exactly is expressed by literature. Literature is now no longer believed to express 'the subject' or 'communal being' – that is, the individuality of the person or of community – but rather the 'sharing of community', that is, its relationality, the fact that community is first of all a matter of relating without our being able to subsume this relationship into some integrative whole. The sharing of community cannot be captured in a word or theory; rather it shows itself in the kind of praxis that consists of nothing other than this sharing 'in and by its writing': the praxis of literature. Writing or reading literature, then, is *the* way to make sense of our contemporary community, because it expresses relationality itself rather than a collective message or collective ideal.[29]

In terms of the symbolic mentioned earlier, we could summarize the essence of the relational paradigm as follows: *the world needs symbolization, not romanticization*. Or in Nancy's words: 'Our task today is nothing less than the task of creating a form or a symbolization of the world.'[30] We should no longer pursue some form of undividedness, some organic whole integrating all parts, but *we should affirm and express that what we call 'world' is, each time, a singularly shared relation*. This task is not about expressing the high hopes of a social ideal, nor is it a pragmatic political programme. It is rather a demand following on from the praxis of literature itself, which is above all a demonstration of the way in which we are in the world – a way that we can call 'precarious' with reference to Bourriaud. After all, what is expressed by literature's mode of being is nothing other than the fact that 'reality', just like 'the world', is not simply given, knowable and identifiable, but is a form of relationality that is created each time anew. Literature does not *represent* this, but makes it happen.[31] If there is indeed still a social relevance to literature, this is what it consists of.

The fragility of literature

An important question in this respect is that of the particularity of literature. After all, if literature is just an expression of the way in which we are in the world, why can't we do without it and just be in the world? And why would it matter at all if we were able to distinguish literature's way of being from other ways of being? As stated earlier, literature not only expresses our relational being in the world, but it also *highlights* this mode of being by demonstrating the practice of relating as such in an exemplary way. Paradoxically, however, it should first of all be recognized as such in order to do so.

The previous two chapters have shown that since Romanticism, demarcating the domain of artistic practices is no easy task. Whereas Kant restricted the aesthetic judgement chiefly to natural objects, the Romantics firmly argued in favour of removing the distinction between art and life, and therefore also between natural and artistic objects – advice that is indeed taken to extremes by Duchamp's ready-mades and Warhol's *Brillo Boxes*. In this respect, modern aesthetics is a clear continuation of Romanticism, as is also highlighted by Loesberg: 'It is precisely the ability to turn the aesthetic perspective on *non-artworks* that … has been its major value for contemporary theory.'[32] Put differently and more bluntly: since the birth of modern aesthetics in Romanticism, the idea that *everything* can become art is its main principle. As we saw, Rancière also recognizes this principle in the aesthetic paradigm and more specifically in the revolutionary literary works of Flaubert and Balzac. Essentially, modern literature should be able to include everything – that is, its 'essence' is to be principally undefined.

The idea that absolute freedom lies at the basis of modern literature and aesthetics is widespread, although sometimes presented in different manifestations. In the case of Thierry De Duve, it is called the '*whatever*' or '*n'importe quoi*': 'what one universally calls art, must be whatever and named as art by whomever. This is the modern imperative stripped bare.'[33] A similar idea is expressed by Jacques Derrida in terms of 'to say everything' or '*tout dire*': 'Literature is a modern invention, it inscribes itself in conventions and institutions which, to hold on to this trait alone, to secure in principle its right to *say everything [le droit de tout dire]*. Literature thus ties its destiny to a certain non-censure, to the space of democratic freedom.'[34] Or, in Rancière's words: 'Art exists as a separate world *since anything whatsoever can belong to it*.'[35] It could indeed be argued that this right to be everything forms the basis of modern literature's autonomy rather than the other way around.³⁶

The notion 'art' is an empty shell – Thierry De Duve formulates this right to be everything in *Kant after Duchamp* (1998). Although it is sometimes rather annoying, the emptiness of this shell does reveal something essential about the *ontological* status of modern art, according to De Duve. In the end it is nothing other than the *name* 'art' that marks the difference between what is art or literature and what is not.³⁷ Of course, attributing this name is not independent of certain preconditions, of more or less well-defined practices as well as some form of consensus, but these preconditions are never decisive: in principle, *everything* can be art.

De Duve calls this a 'nominalist ontology' and argues that it is most clearly exemplified by Duchamp's – or rather Elsa von Freytag-Loringhoven's – *Fountain*. This pioneering work has proven that even a urinal can be art if artists and museum visitors are willing to call it that, for whatever reason.

> This particular urinal has nothing in common with any of the countless things carrying the name of art, except that it is, like them, called art. And nothing distinguishes it from any ordinary urinal, from non-art, except, once again, its name, art. In conclusion, it allows you to administer the striking proof of art's very autonomy, taking the glorious form of a *nominalist ontology*.³⁸

Albeit in a less iconic way, Dada or, more recently, Flarf poetry, demonstrates that literature, too, needs to be claimed and re-invented time and again because it does not refer to an objectively definable reality. As soon as it is claimed, the name 'literature' nevertheless radically changes the *way* a text exists for us according to this nominalist ontology: lines from a newspaper article *exist* differently when they are part of a press article than when they are read as poetry.

However, if everything can potentially be considered literary, what does this literariness consist of? In what way does the *way* in which a text exists for us change when it receives the name 'literature'? The answer I have given so far is that literature is unique in enabling the ontological structure of our being in the world to be revealed. We should, however, add here that literature's revelation works in a quite specific way. In order to unpack the peculiarities of this revelation, the work of Blanchot is most welcome. Paradoxically, Blanchot observes in 'Literature and the Right to Death' (1949), literature reveals the world's ontological structure by making the world first of all *unreal*. In other words, it brackets the world – not by replacing it by another, imaginary, world but by making the world's reality *itself* unreal. This is what Blanchot calls literature's capacity for 'global negation':

> What can a writer do? Everything. ... [But] the truth is that the writer also ruins action, not because he deals with what is unreal, but because he makes all of reality available to us. Unreality begins with the whole. The realm of the imaginary is not a strange region situated beyond the world, it is the world itself, but the world as entire, manifold, the world as a whole ... . It is the world, grasped and realized in its entirety by the global negation of all the individual realities contained in it, by their disqualification, their absence ... which is where literary creation begins.[39]

As is stated by Blanchot, a de-realization of the real by literature boils down to a disqualification of the established facticity of reality. This global negation does not imply that literary writers retreat from the world, nor that they change it, since both moves only make sense on an ontic level, that is, as a retreat from or intervention in specific norms, practices or institutions that precisely make up the facticity of reality.

The de-realization peculiar to literature is more fundamental and, indeed, global. It is the disqualification of the world in its entirety and is, therefore, the creation in the world of a moment of full potential, a moment when everything seems possible. Conceptually, Blanchot compares literary creation with the moment of revolution. Like a revolution, literature is the creation of this one interstitial instant, where, with the king beheaded and time suspended, suddenly *everything* is possible. This is the miracle of literature's ontological nature, Blanchot maintains: 'If literature coincides with nothing for just an instant, it is immediately everything, and this everything begins to exist: what a miracle!'[40] Literature, then, is a means to unhinge the established facticity of daily reality and to turn it into full potentiality, to turn the exclamation mark usually accompanying our being in the world into a question mark.

This bracketing of reality as such, of reality *in its totality*, is literature's miraculous power, but also, as Blanchot argues, its weakness. By making the totality of the world available to us as something that can be recreated according to one's own will, this totality at the same time loses its self-evidence: the real being de-realized. Even if the literary world created is similar in almost every respect to the actual one, as in realist fiction, the fact that the writer *could have* created a completely different world means that its value in terms of reality is put at stake. This is the experience evoked, to varying degrees, by all texts that we call literary, varying from historical novels to avant-garde poetry, from literary thrillers to post-modernist fiction. The result of the fact that the creative freedom of modern literature resides in the possibility of recreating *everything* is that what is actually created comes across *as unreal* because it could just as well have been completely different.

Although in modernity everything can in principle be turned into literature, a more or less deliberate decision needs, of course, to be taken in order to do so. For something to exist *as* literature, it first needs to be considered as such. This is the paradox of modern literature's open definition: since there is no clear-cut dividing line separating literature from non-literature, a text only constitutes itself as literature in the act of writing or reading it as such – a groundless decision that will subsequently be of influence in future moments of groundless self-affirmation. In other words, the very basic judgement 'this is literature' precedes any other judgement concerning, for instance, a literary work's genre or style. What is important is that it is by no means the text's *quality* that is concerned here. Whether something should be considered good or bad literature is a different and, in this respect, secondary issue. The basic aesthetic judgement 'this is literature' is a performative judgement that only concerns the *quod* of literature – *that* it is – and not the *quid* – *what* it is. Or put differently: it is a constitutive judgement, not a normative one.

Of course, there are wide-ranging factors that invite us to consider a specific work as literary, from textual properties to the way authors present themselves and their work, to the influence of sociocultural institutions. For something, however, actually to exist *as* literature, that is, as something that de-realizes the real, our attitude towards the text is decisive. The reader who reads Dostoyevsky's *The House of the Dead* as an historical reconstruction of life in a Siberian prison camp, or Daniel Defoe's *Robinson Crusoe* as the report of a solitary expedition is, although completely legitimized to do so, *not* reading it as a piece of literature. Considering literature as a specific mode of existence rather than as a product or state of affairs means that to begin with, one conceives of the world evoked as a form of de-realization, that is, as the total negation of the actual world by means of the creation of an imaginary world that may or may not be consistent with our conception of the actual world.

In doing so, it is not only the writer, but also society and the readers that take responsibility for literature – not for its content, but for its *existence*.[41] The future role of literature in society is thus partly dependent on the willingness of readers to bear this responsibility – a willingness that can be stimulated by policy, education or training. After all, the main consequence of the relational paradigm is that literature does not exist once and for all as a solid entity: it happens each time anew, and might just as well not happen. This is to say that works are not intrinsically literary, but *become* literary in interaction. In this sense, every work of art, even a literary one, should be called 'participatory', since it requires a receiver in order to exist, not as an artefact, but *as* literature.

One of the most powerful aspects of this paradigm of relationality is that it reveals the extreme fragility of literature: as soon as one decides *not* to consider something as literature, it ceases to work that way. This is why, for instance, Ayatolla Khomeini could refuse to read *The Satanic Verses* as literature. However, it also increases our own responsibility as (professional) readers and society. Since it is the judgement 'this is literature' that brings it into existence, literature's death knell is thus only to be feared when we ourselves decide to turn our back on it. Obviously, this has important consequences for the very idea of literary commitment.

Commitment: The ontic approach

As we saw earlier, despite their differences, the shared conviction between autonomists and anti-autonomists is the idea that literature is relevant to society. Whether this relevance is attributed to the committed writer who ideologically intervenes in the public sphere, or rather to some form of neutral detachment or idiosyncrasy – both autonomists and anti-autonomists are driven by a firm belief in the fact that we are better off *with* literature than without it. But what exactly is its social relevance?

In ontic theories, this relevance is often described in terms of a particular social or moral commitment. This does not necessarily concern the transmission of moral lessons or universal values, but rather the development of a particular ethical sensitivity, the ability to behave responsibly in society, the denunciation of abuses or the overall concern for fellow human beings. According to this view, reading fiction develops feelings of empathy, compassion or solidarity and provides insight into lives and situations with which we are less familiar. Literature *as literature* is, according to this ontic approach, the best way to develop these ethical competencies, because literature involves a sensitivity that cannot be developed by a purely political, journalistic or scientific discourse.

Although this ontic approach certainly has its value, it must be distinguished from the approach following on from the relational paradigm developed in this book. To clarify the difference between the two, I shall proceed first with the ontic approach of literature's social relevance. Although many would primarily associate this view with theories such as those of Martha Nussbaum, one of the most careful elaborations of this view can be found in Richard Rorty's *Contingency, Irony, and Solidarity* (1989).

Rorty situates the question of literature's social relevance within the broader context of Western intellectual history. About two hundred years ago, he asserts, we started to realize that truth was something *made* rather than *found*.[42] Ultimately, both truth and the social values ensuing from it are considered to be *contingent*, that is, historically determined and changeable. According to Rorty, two important questions arise in this situation, questions the interconnectedness of which he elaborates upon: 1) how is *solidarity* still possible in this situation and 2) what role can *literature* play in achieving it?

The key term for him in both cases is *cruelty*. When society itself, as well as our ideas about society and the words with which we formulate these ideas are contingent, there is, Rorty maintains, only one important test case that can be taken as the basis for the way we shape society: avoiding cruelty.[43] In the end, this should be *the* basic principle in a society that tries to face the contingency of existence. This directive would enable modern human beings to embrace the contingency of their own central beliefs while at the same time seeking to reduce the suffering of others.[44] According to Rorty, literature is crucial to the success of this enterprise because people today can no longer subscribe to universal ideals or truths. Solidarity is therefore 'to be achieved not by inquiry but by *imagination*, the imaginative ability to see strange people as fellow sufferers'.[45]

Rorty considers the novel to be excellently equipped for such a task, because it enables one to sympathize with the suffering of others, even when they are distant from us. Whereas philosophical theories often run the risk of forgetting their own relativism, novels, in Rorty's words, are 'a *safer* medium than theory for expressing one's recognition of the relativity and contingency of authority figures. For novels are usually about people – things which are ... quite evidently time-bound, embedded in a web of contingencies'.[46] Because novelists use their imagination to make the suffering of real people in real situations understandable without making a claim to the general validity of their depiction, it is indeed *as writers*, Rorty argues, that these novelists are the most suitable social counsellors of our time.

In this respect, Rorty opposes himself to those who claim that literature can only be of social importance when its aesthetic value is secondary to its ethical message. The key role Rorty has in mind for the literary writer implies that we need to break with the persistent distinction between ethics and aesthetics. Not only can novels with a clear moral message play a role in a person's *Bildung*, but also novels that might be called purely aesthetic according to this obsolete conceptual opposition, such as those of Nabokov. In the latter case, Rorty describes the moral relevance as a *lesson in autonomy*, that is: a lesson in finding one's place in a contingent world, with one's own contingent, idiosyncratic beliefs. Because virtually every novel gives an insight into the specific circumstances of another life, virtually every novel will create sensitivity to the contingency of one's own existence. This mere sensitivity alone has a moral relevance according to Rorty. After all, understanding the contingency of one's own existence will imply that one will not impose one's own views at all costs on others.

Rorty therefore suggests replacing the distinction between the ethical and the aesthetic by a distinction between two kinds of ethical aesthetics: one being a lesson in autonomy and one being a lesson in cruelty: 'As traditionally employed, by both "moralists" and "aesthetics", that [moral and aesthetic, AvR] distinction merely blurs the distinction I am trying to draw between relevance to autonomy and relevance to cruelty.'[47] In times like ours, where there are no longer universal values to be proclaimed by writers, Rorty emphasizes that both kinds of lessons are required. Both the idiosyncratic literary universes of Nabokov and the politically charged ones of Orwell, therefore, are socially relevant. Or at least this is what Rorty *wants* to claim. In the end, however, he has to conclude more or less in spite of himself that the first type of novel only has private, but no *social* relevance, which largely undermines his own attack on the distinction between ethics and aesthetics.

Rorty's view reveals a contradiction that seems to be characteristic of all ontic approaches to the social relevance of literature. Although literature's social relevance is initially attributed to the phenomenon of literature *as literature*, it is eventually found only in literary works of a *particular kind*. In Rorty's view, the reduction of cruelty should not only be taken as a guideline in politics, but also in determining the social relevance of novels he considers to be self-evident when there is a question of cruelty.[48] Avoiding cruelty is thus the basis for Rorty's central distinction between 'books that help us to become autonomous' and 'books that help us to become less cruel'. Where the first type of books is relevant to the development of the *private self*, the second one is '*relevant to our relations with others*' and therefore relevant in the public domain.[49] *All* literature – irrespective of the kind of novel – may be of a certain importance for us; in the light of Rorty's political theory, the dichotomy between two kinds of novels ultimately appears to be a hierarchy.

Because solidarity with the suffering of others has been Rorty's main concern from the outset, the first type of novels – the autonomous ones – can only appear as less relevant within this approach. When cruelty is taken as the unwavering touchstone, Rorty not only *can* make a clear distinction between works that denounce cruelty and works that do not, but it would also be unethical if he were not to do so. The message, or at least the novel's theme, is decisive here, decisive even in the sense that works within the category of novels 'relevant to cruelty' are subdivided according to their themes: 'The books which help us to become less cruel', as Rorty continues his analysis,

> can be roughly divided into (1) books which help us to see the effects of social practices and institutions on others and (2) those which help us to see the effects of our private idiosyncrasies on others. The first sort of book is typified by books about, for example, slavery, poverty, and prejudice … the second sort of book … is about the ways in which particular sorts of people are cruel to other particular sorts of people.[50]

Although initially, Rorty seemed to situate the social relevance of literature in its *mode of existence*, which he described as 'safer' than that of theoretical discourse, he eventually identifies it with the work's *message* and, in doing so, even completely drops the distinction previously made between literature and theory. As examples of books that help us to see the effects of social practices and institutions, Rorty mentions not only *Uncle Tom's Cabin*, but also Friedrich Engels's *The Condition of the Working Class in England* and 'the reports of muckraking journalists and government commissions'.[51] In the end, the difference between literary and non-literary texts seems therefore to be only a matter of scale: because novels can describe things at greater length, they can bring cruelty to the fore more vividly.

Although Rorty's view of literature is only one among many, his view exposes a contradiction that is inherent in all ontic views of the social relevance of literature. Since this relevance is situated in a particular ethical effect (e.g. 'helping to see the effects of social practices on others'), a distinction has to be made between different kinds of literary works, be it a categorical division or a gradual one, running from socially irrelevant to socially relevant literature. This holds true not only for Rorty's distinction between 'books relevant to autonomy' and 'books relevant to cruelty', but also for the influential distinction Milan Kundera makes in *The Art of the Novel* (that partly inspired Rorty) between 'novelists who are after a form' and 'writers who have original ideas', for the distinction Todorov (who is inspired by Rorty) makes between an 'internal approach' and an 'external approach', as well as for the distinction Nussbaum makes between novels that prioritize 'the particular' and those that give priority to 'the general'.[52]

The division between socially relevant and socially irrelevant literature causes the above-mentioned ontic approaches to remain stuck within the outdated opposition that they aimed to overcome: that between aesthetics and ethics, autonomy and commitment. In the relational paradigm, however, it is the existence of the phenomenon of literature as such – that is to say, of *all possible* literature – that is considered relevant for society.

Commitment: An ontological approach

The reason why, from an ontic perspective, we cannot succeed in overcoming the persistent modern opposition between aesthetics and ethics, autonomy and commitment, art and life, has to do with *the way in which* the question of literature's social relevance is posed. Generally, this question takes the following form '*What purposes does this book serve?*'[53] Contrary to what one might expect, it is not so much the *purpose* attributed to literature which renders this question inappropriate, but the fact that this purpose is attributed to '*this book*'. Within the relational paradigm, the social relevance is not something to be attributed to the characteristics of one novel –

to its theme, its persuasiveness or the biography of its author – but to *literature as such*, that is, to *the existence of the phenomenon of literature*.

To ask about the social relevance of literature is therefore not to ask: 'What purpose does this book serve?', but to ask '*What purpose does the existence of literature serve?*' In order to disclose the potential social relevance of literature from this angle, we must return to what is unique to the literary perspective, a perspective that, as we noted earlier with Blanchot, consists of a de-realization of reality. In what sense can this de-realization be of social or even ethical importance? Is it not rather the source of the dreaded moral indifference, the despised *anything goes* often associated with contemporary literature? Does the writer's absolute freedom involved in this de-realization not result in a creation that is utterly vain, empty and without obligation? Yes. However, if the creative freedom of literature were not *absolute* and were restricted to works, for instance, that broach certain social issues or provide a certain insight, literature would lose the social power precisely brought about by its *global* negation, by creating that limbo where *everything* is possible.

The social relevance of this absolute freedom lies in the awareness of what I have called the ontological precariousness of existence, the awareness that life has no definitive form. For Bourriaud, the notion of 'precariousness' was mainly a way to describe the ever-changing and fluid world of the contemporary cosmopolitan internet user, but as we have seen, this also applies to our more general human condition as described by post-structuralist and deconstructivist theories. The precariousness indicates that our world is, time and again, a singular form of connectedness that can never be determined in its entirety. An infinite becoming, to quote the Romantics, but without direction or progression. Although in our everyday being in the world, this sense of precariousness is hidden behind the normal course of life, literature unhinges this everydayness – it de-realizes reality.

To use a Blanchotian terminology once again, we could say that literature opens up to 'the other of all worlds': 'Though the work there takes place in time another time, and in the world of beings that exist, and of things which subsist, there comes, as presence, not another world, but the other of all worlds, that which is always other than the world.'[54] The distinction between 'another world' and 'the other of all worlds' is important because it forms the basis of the difference between an ontic and an ontological approach to literature. Those who discuss the merits and demerits of literature's autonomy usually conceive of literature as the opening of another world, of a world separate from ours that satisfies our need to escape reality, or that discloses what otherwise might have remained hidden.

The 'other of all worlds', however, is something different. Certainly, reading or writing means in a sense to withdraw from everyday life. When reading a book, in a way another world, or another space and time, opens up within ordinary reality. While reading Pamuk's *My Name is Red* on a warm spring evening in 2018 on the couch, the cat curled on my lap, I suddenly find myself in the studio of a miniature painter on a winter morning in sixteenth-century Istanbul. But this is in no way *another world*, another separate and isolated one from my own world. After all, the literary world opened up by this book has none of the characteristics a *reality* should have for it to be called that, like material presence, spatial dimensions, or living inhabitants. To the extent that these characteristics are evoked, they are done so in a de-realized way, as mentioned earlier. To quote the above-cited passage from Blanchot again: 'The realm of the imaginary is not a strange region situated beyond the world, it is the world itself, but the world as entire, manifold, the world as a whole.'[55]

Literature is a special, de-realized way of being. It opens up a form of being in the world that is located at a vanishing point, at the point at which connections are made, in which (the) world is created as being, time and again, a set of relations in which and by which we live. Literature is, in other words, a form of being in the world that is at the same time inside and outside 'the' world. Or, as Nancy puts it in *The Muses* (2001): literature is the '*coming* of the world', its origin, its creation: 'What has no place *in* the world is the coming of the world, its event. In a sense this is nothing other than the world itself ... the fact *that there is world*.'[56]

Since 'the' world is not an object that came into existence in some immemorial past, but is constantly coming into existence, it is re-emerging time and again. The cat on my lap suddenly gets an unsuspected inner life because of the talking animals in Pamuk's novel, the roaring cars outside my window get the chilly sound of a harsh winter storm, and my Western perception of visual culture is gaining depth by being placed in oriental perspective. The coming of the world, its event, is only possible from this peculiar de-realized mode of existence, because it entails a viewpoint of its totality, of the world 'as a whole'. Again, what is at stake is not the creation of some other world, besides or behind the real one, but the creation of the other of all worlds, that is, of the unhinging of my 'worldliness' as the established facticity of given states of affairs.

This mode of being is paradoxical and difficult to conceptualize, but when put into an historical perspective, it is nothing but the all too familiar mode of being of the Christian monotheistic God, the ultimate Creator, being both outside and inside the world, at its origin. One could say that at the beginning of modernity – accompanied by the beginning of modern literature – this divine mode of being has been brought *into* the world. Literature is the exceptional event where this absolute creative outside can take place at the very heart of being, in the everydayness of the world. It is a being at the margins of our being in the world, at the point where its creation is made perceivable and sensible. The literary mode of being is therefore in no way superficial, indifferent or without obligation. It is a way of being in the world in which connections are made and values created, a way of being in which, time and again, a world is formed.

Although Rorty or Nussbaum, too, among others, would describe literature as a way of unhinging the self-evident frameworks that make up our ordinary reality, their ontic approach differs in one important respect from the ontological approach proposed here. Certainly, a novel by Pamuk does actually disrupt the horizon of expectation of many a contemporary Western reader and can thereby create a certain sensitivity to what eludes one's social, cultural and historical frame of reference. This is, however, not an ontological, but a *cultural* or even *epistemological* form of disruption. Since this disruption is negatively dependent on the given socio-cultural-historical constellation, only a very few literary works are able to perform such a disruption and, moreover, only in the case of a limited number of readers. Works that fully comply with our formal or thematic expectations are deprived of this disruptive power. Indeed, literature is exceptionally effective in bringing across what eludes our socio-cultural-historical frame of reference. But if literature's social relevance were limited to this ability, we should either conclude that only a very few literary works are of social importance, or that it is not so much the phenomenon of literature as such that has social relevance, but only certain texts dealing with certain issues in a certain way.

By contrast, the ontological approach to literature's social relevance concerns all works that we tend to call literary, varying from clichéd genre writing to modernist prose, from sound poetry to historical novels. As I have indicated, the crux of the relational approach lies in our engagement with the phenomenon of literature, regardless of style, theme or genre. The sensitivity raised by its mode of existence is not sensitivity to the unfamiliar, but to the contingency of the most ordinary. In other words, the disruption in and by literature is, according to the relational paradigm, not cultural or epistemological, but primarily ontological.

The other of all worlds opened up in reading or writing literature is not a radically different world. It is the opening up or the happening of the world itself, of this world, my world. Understood from the perspective of the relational paradigm, literature is not an event of the *alius* or *alienus* being opposed to what is proper, but that of the *alter*, the alternative, the alternating. Literature is not what disrupts the self by showing the other-than-self, but is what shows the incessant-otherness-of-the-self, my world being different all the time.[57]

This creation of relationships that literature is, is singular, each and every time anew. Not only is every poem or novel unique in its creation of a meaningful web of relations, but the novel I read last night in bed also relates in a different way to the same novel I read today during my daily commute by train. In other words, on Sunday evening the 'same' novel *exists differently* than on Monday morning, not only because it is part of a different reading experience, but because this reading experience is part of another world and creates another world. Within the relational paradigm, literature is therefore not separate from, or even *opposed* to, the recognizable world, but expresses the continuous singular and plural act of relating that is (the) world. If literature has a social or moral lesson to teach, it consists of this very basic insight that what we call 'world' is different all the time. It is the extrapolation of this ontological conception of our being in the world to the field of literary theory that might help overcome the unfruitful modern dualism between text and context.

Towards a new form of literary criticism

With the relational paradigm outlined in this chapter, I have tried to develop, mainly on the basis of developments in twentieth and twenty-first-century post-structuralist philosophy, a new theoretical framework for understanding literature and its role in society. As mentioned earlier, it does not present an entirely new view on literary autonomy and commitment, but is an attempt to reassess the main aspirations of the Romantic paradigm – the aspirations that have led to the birth of modern literature – in a manner consistent with recent developments in Western thought. With this re-assessment, I wanted to avoid two things. Firstly, the impression that the relational paradigm replacing the Romantic paradigm would be a revolutionary new beginning, putting all past ideas behind us. I have therefore not only emphasized the continuity between the aspirations underlying the Romantic and the relational paradigm, but also the fact that the latter concurs with some general developments in philosophy and philosophically inspired disciplines.

The second impression that I wanted to avoid is the opposite impression that the relational paradigm is merely a continuation of the Romantic paradigm by other means, or old wine in new bottles. The basic principles of both paradigms differ greatly, and the collapse of the Romantic paradigm necessitated the formulation of a new one. Although the relational ontology central to the relational paradigm reflects and elaborates the Romantic pursuit of overcoming the opposition between autonomy and social engagement on an ontological level, it also reflects, as I have argued, a fundamental shift in intellectual history from the absolute to the contingent, from the principle of individuality to the principle of relationality.

In doing so, the relational paradigm provides the theoretical framework for a form of literary criticism that understands literature prior to, or beyond, the paralyzing dualisms of autonomy and commitment, aesthetics and ethics, text and context. Unfortunately, but necessarily, the ontological approach presented by this paradigm resists an elaboration in terms of a practical method or investigative principles. A slightly different approach is therefore required to the one to which we were accustomed in the post-Romantic debates between autonomists and anti-autonomists.

Firstly, the relational paradigm is at odds with the current categorization of academic disciplines. To understand the contemporary social function of literature, not only is an inter-, trans- or multi-disciplinary approach required, but more importantly an approach that also transgresses the existing academic fields. As we saw earlier, the polemic between autonomists and anti-autonomists is rooted within the dualistic framework that characterizes modernity as such. Since academic fields such as the sociology of literature, postcolonial studies, reception theory, New Criticism, and New Formalism have emerged from this dualistic framework, a relational approach to literature developed *from within* one of these fields of study is bound to fail. Attempts to redefine literature's role within the contemporary world necessarily break down at the boundaries of these disciplines. Although it is difficult to venture beyond the borders between these disciplines when they are still firmly in place, this is one of the main challenges of future debate concerning literature in contemporary society.

The same holds true for the boundaries between national literatures. In literature departments all over the world, the study of literature is traditionally divided into national literatures. This division might make sense from a historical and nationalist perspective, but from a literary perspective it really does not. Viewed from a relational perspective, the language in which a work is written is only of secondary importance. Although literature's effect is highly dependent on the text and thus on the language in which this text is written, the specific language is just one among many factors for understanding the way a literary text works. As we saw earlier, within the relational paradigm, literature is not so much the product of a certain historical or sociocultural background, but is a specific mode of existence evoked by the way in which a literary text exists, as the creation of a singular and unique relation, with each reading anew, in translation too.

This does not imply, however, that the issues of literature, autonomy and commitment should be examined from a global perspective. On the contrary. Usually, such a global perspective results either in a consolidation of the national perspectives by means of some form of comparative literary studies, or in a homogenization of the perspective in which literature is considered according to a more or less uniform genesis of a 'World Republic of Letters'.[58] Viewed from a relational paradigm, these issues should instead be approached in a casuistic way, in which a literary work is not perceived as *representative* of a larger subset, but as a unique case. To concur with De Duve: what we call literature should not be taken as a generic name or a family name, but as a *proper name*, a name which, although it occurs frequently, nevertheless always refers to a strictly unique case, the uniqueness of which should first and foremost also be examined.[59] The significance of that uniqueness lies, however, in a relational way of being that might also consist of the connection created by a certain language, nationality, generation or community. In examining the way contemporary literature works from a relational perspective, these collective identities can never, however, be taken as a point of departure.

The final and perhaps greatest challenge concerns the academic stature of such a study. During the past few decades, literary studies have opted for an increasingly empirical approach modelled on the natural sciences, which is the case, for instance, in empirical literary studies and computational models working with big data. This empirical approach undoubtedly has its merits, not least of which is a consolidation within the academic landscape. However, it is also one of the main causes of what I have described as the 'forgetfulness of literature', that is, the forgetfulness of the mode of being of what we call literature. Since the relational paradigm wishes to touch upon this mode of being, a different and, in the eyes of some, perhaps less academic approach is needed: not so much an empirical or objective attempt to define, classify and quantify literary products, but a more casuistic, phenomenological or hermeneutical approach that does justice to the uniqueness of literary works rather than the ability to generalize.

When one wishes to examine the characteristics of a text, an author or an institutional context, an objectifying approach is certainly an appropriate one. However, when one wishes to grasp the peculiar significance of the way in which literature interacts with our contemporary lives, the second type of approach is required. As we saw, literature understood as a relational phenomenon is not only dynamic and changeable but is also highly dependent on the involvement of the reader. To theorize, define and classify literature is only possible when this dynamic event is brought to a standstill, momentarily interrupted, in the hope that a glimpse of it can be recaptured in theory. This is not entirely impossible, and this final chapter is an attempt to do this. Nevertheless, examining the social role of literature requires a certain modesty. Literature is primarily something one should *do* and, only to a very small extent, something about which one can theorize.

By meeting these challenges, the relational paradigm provides a framework that can turn the fruitless debate between autonomists and anti-autonomists into a more fruitful one. This does not necessarily mean that the autonomy debate is brought to a conclusion, just that other issues may prove to be more essential. The urgency of the autonomy debate will change overall. Navigating between the ruins of Romanticism, the autonomy debate had for centuries the maximum possible stake: the survival of literature. Both the autonomists' and the anti-autonomists' goal was to save literature from its imminent death. That looming abyss caused a large part of the fire and urgency of the debate. Terms like 'danger', 'firing back', 'defence', 'return' and 'manifesto' have all derived their strength from this conjured abyss.[60]

Within the framework of the relational paradigm, this abyss appears to be largely an optical illusion caused by the distorted perspective of a past paradigm, and rescuing literature from it seems decidedly less urgent. The opposition between autonomists and anti-autonomists is thereby not dissolved but shifts in its focus. Because this opposition is no longer motivated by the sacred duty to save literature from its demise, the claims raised by autonomists and anti-autonomists will represent different dimensions of the multifaceted phenomenon of literature rather than mutually exclusive principles. It may take some time to get used to a debate focused on nuance and consensus rather than on controversy, but it may very well provide a sustainable framework for future literary criticism.

Notes

Introduction

1. See, for example, Alvin Kernan, *The Death of Literature* (New Haven/London: Yale University Press, 1990); John Martin Ellis, *Literature Lost: Social Agendas and the Corruption of the Humanities* (New Haven/London: Yale University Press, 1997); Richard A. Posner, *Public Intellectuals: A Study of Decline* (Cambridge, MA: Harvard University Press, 2002); Gayatri Spivak, *Death of a Discipline* (New York: Columbia University Press, 2003); William Marx, *L'Adieu à la littérature: Histoire d'une dévalorisation, XVIIIe–XXe siècles* (Paris: Minuit, 2005); Tzvetan Todorov, *La littérature en péril* (Paris: Flammarion, 2007); Antoine Compagnon, *Littérature, pour quoi faire?* (Paris: Fayard/Collège de France, 2007); and Ronan McDonald, *Death of the Critic* (London: Continuum, 2007).
2. Marx, *L'Adieu à la littérature*, 12. Translations are mine.
3. Ibid., 12.
4. Ibid., 168.
5. Ibid., 61.
6. Ibid., 18.
7. Ibid., 60.
8. Ibid., 13.
9. Theodor Dalrymple, *Our Culture, What's Left of It: The Mandarins and the Masses* (Chicago: Ivan R. Dee, 2005).
10. Marx, *L'Adieu à la littérature*, 180–1.
11. Ibid., 167.
12. Jonathan D. Fitzgerald, 'Sincerity, Not Irony, Is Our Age's Ethos', *The Atlantic*, 20 November 2012.
13. Roger Rosenblatt, 'The Age of Irony Comes to an End', *Time Magazine*, 24 September 2001. See for later reiterations of this observation Zoe Williams, 'The Final Irony', *The Guardian*, 28 June 2003; and Michael

Hirschorn, 'Irony, The End of: Why Graydon Carter Wasn't Entirely Wrong', *New Yorker Magazine*, 27 August 2011.

14 See, for example, Allard den Dulk, *Existentialist Engagement in Wallace, Eggers and Foer: A Philosophical Analysis of Contemporary American Literature* (New York: Bloomsbury, 2015); and Ellen Rutten, *Sincerity after Communism: A Cultural History* (New Haven: Yale University Press, 2017).

15 See, for example, Nicoline Timmer, *Do You Feel It Too? The Post-Postmodern Syndrome in American Fiction at the Turn of the Millennium* (Amsterdam: Rodopi, 2010); Timotheus Vermeulen and Robin van den Akker, 'Notes on Metamodernism', *Journal of Aesthetics and Culture* 2 (2010): 1–14; Mary K. Holland, *Succeeding Postmodernism: Language and Humanism in Contemporary American Literature* (New York: Bloomsbury, 2014); Irmtraud Huber, *Literature after Postmodernism: Reconstructive Fantasies* (New York: Palgrave Macmillan, 2014); and Lee Konstantinou, *Cool Characters* (Cambridge, MA: Harvard University Press, 2016). For an overview of twentieth- and twenty-first-century post-postmodernist movements, see Jon Doyle, 'The Changing Face of Post-Postmodern Fiction: Irony, Sincerity, and Populism', *Critique* 59.3 (2018): 259–70.

16 Rita Felski, *Uses of Literature* (Oxford: Blackwell, 2008), 132.

17 Felski, *Uses of Literature*, 22.

18 Rita Felski, *The Limits of Critique* (Chicago: University of Chicago Press, 2015), 172.

19 Felski, *Uses of Literature*, 2. See also Stella Butler, 'A Manifesto for Positive Aesthetics' (review of: Felski, *Uses of Literature*), in: *Online Journal of Literary Theory* (2009).

20 Felski, *Uses of Literature*, 13–14. According to Felski, these cognitive and affective modes of engagement loosely refer to the aesthetic categories of anagnorisis, beauty, mimesis and the sublime.

21 Felski, *The Limits of Critique*, 160–1 and 180. Italics are mine.

22 Todorov, *La littérature en peril*, 72. Translations are mine.

23 Ibid., 85.

24 Ibid., 90.

25 Caroline Levine, *Forms: Whole, Rhythm, Hierarchy, Network* (Princeton: Princeton University Press, 2015). For recent contributions to the New Formalist debate, see also the 2017 Autumn issue of *Critical Inquiry*, containing responses to Jonathan Kramnick and Anahid Nersessian's 'Form and Explanation', *Critical Inquiry* 43 (Spring 2017): 650–69.
26 Levine, *Forms*, xii.
27 Marx, *L'Adieu à la littérature*, 180.
28 Jonathan Loesberg, *A Return to Aesthetics: Autonomy, Indifference, and Postmodernism* (Stanford: Stanford University Press, 2005); Gregory Jusdanis, *Fiction Agonistes: In Defense of Literature* (Stanford: Stanford University Press, 2010); and Andrew Goldstone, *Fictions of Autonomy: From Wilde to De Man* (Oxford: Oxford University Press, 2013).
29 Pierre Bourdieu, *Firing Back: Against the Tyranny of the Market 2* (New York: Verso, 2003), 12.
30 Bourdieu, *Firing Back 2*, 66.
31 Ibid., 67.
32 Ibid., 73.
33 Ibid., 18.
34 Ibid.
35 Ibid.
36 Ibid., 81.
37 Ibid., 20.
38 Ibid., 38.
39 Ibid., 25.
40 Theodor Adorno, *Aesthetic Theory* (New York: Bloomsbury, 1997), 79.
41 Adorno, *Aesthetic Theory*, 79.
42 See also Theodor Adorno, 'Commitment', in *Notes to Literature*, vol. 2 (New York: Columbia University Press, 1992).
43 Adorno, *Aesthetic Theory*, 3.
44 Ibid., 308.
45 Ibid.
46 Ibid., 342: 'The double character of art – something that severs itself from empirical reality and thereby from society's functional context and yet is at the same time part of empirical reality and society's functional

context – is directly apparent in the aesthetic phenomena, which are both aesthetic and *faits sociaux*.'

47 Adorno, *Aesthetic Theory*, 5.
48 R. Jay Magill Jr., *Sincerity: How a Moral Ideal Born Five Hundred Years Ago also Inspired Religious Wars, Modern Art...* (New York: W.W. Norton & Co., 2012), 223.
49 Elke D'hoker and Gunther Martens (eds), *Narrative Unreliability in the Twentieth-Century First-Person Novel* (Berlin: Walter de Gruyter, 2008).
50 See also Johannes Voelz about New Sincerity: 'Irony here becomes a particular mode of sincerity'. Johannes Voelz, 'The New Sincerity as Literary Hospitality', in Jeffrey Clapp and Emily Ridge (eds), *Security and Hospitality in Literature and Culture* (New York: Routledge, 2015), 216.
51 Ernst van Alphen, Mieke Bal and Carel E. Smith, *The Rhetoric of Sincerity* (New York: Stanford University Press, 2009), 3.
52 Doyle, 'The Changing Face of Post-Postmodernist Fiction', 268.
53 Gregory Jusdanis, 'Two Cheers for Aesthetic Autonomy', *Cultural Critique* 61 (2005): 22–54, here: 28–9. Or as the title of Caroline Levine's contribution to one of the most recent manifestations of this tug-of-war succinctly puts it: 'Still Polemicizing After All These Years'. Levine's contribution is a response to Jonathan Krammick and Anahid Nersessian's polemic article 'Form and Explanation', 650–69. In the same issue, Tom Eyers, too, underlines that 'one rather feels that we've been here before'. Tom Eyers, 'Critical Response II: Theory over Method, or In Defense of Polemic', *Critical Inquiry* 44 (Autumn 2017): 140.
54 Jusdanis, 'Two Cheers for Aesthetic Autonomy', 30.
55 Ibid., 32.
56 See, for instance, Simon Critchley, *The Ethics of Deconstruction: Derrida and Levinas* (New York: Blackwell, 1992).
57 Noël Carroll, 'At the Crossroads of Ethics and Aesthetics', *Philosophy and Literature* 34 (2010): 248–59.
58 Tony Bennett, 'Sociology, Aesthetics, Expertise', *New Literary History* 41 (2010): 251–76; and Gregory Jusdanis, 'Two Cheers for Aesthetic Autonomy', in *Fiction Agonistes*.

59 Goldstone, *Fictions of Autonomy*, 4. The 'four classes' of autonomy distinguished by Goldstone are subsequently autonomy from labour, autonomy from the person, expatriation as autonomy, and autonomy from an external reference.

60 Emmett Stinson, *Satirizing Modernism: Aesthetic Autonomy, Romanticism, and the Avant-Garde* (New York: Bloomsbury, 2017), 3–8.

61 Loesberg, *A Return to Aesthetics*. For an overview of the recent scholarly debate, see Gregory Jusdanis' lengthy article, 'Two Cheers for Aesthetic Autonomy'; and the introduction to Stinson's *Satirizing Modernism*.

Chapter 1

1 Rüdiger Safranski, *Romanticism: A German Affair* (Evanston: Northwestern University Press, 2014), 140. Italics are mine.

2 Frederick C. Beiser, *The Romantic Imperative: The Concept of Early German Romanticism* (Cambridge, MA: Harvard University Press, 2003), 186: 'The problems that so troubled the Romantics – the sources of torment behind all their sleepless nights – are still with us'. And Maarten Doorman: 'If we discuss Western art of today, we discuss Romantic art … Romanticism has been constitutive for art practices for two centuries now: its influence is everywhere.' Maarten Doorman, 'Persistent Autonomy and Romanticism', *Aesthetic Investigations* 1.1 (2015): 77. Translation slightly modified. For a more elaboration analysis of the omnipresent influence of Romanticism in contemporary aesthetic discourse, see Doorman's book *De Romantische orde* [The Romantic Order] (Amsterdam: Bert Bakker, 2004). In *Romanticism*, Hugh Honour even asserts that 'Romantic ideas and concepts are so deeply embedded in our attitudes and ways of thinking about art that we are rarely aware of them'. Hugh Honour, *Romanticism* (Harmondsworth: Penguin Books, 1991), 319.

3 Jacques Rancière, *The Politics of Aesthetics: The Distribution of the Sensible* (New York: Bloomsbury, 2004), 7–14. For a more elaborate

account of the three regimes with regard to literature, see Rancière, *Mute Speech* (2011) and Rancière, *The Politics of Literature* (2011).

4 Rancière, *The Politics of Aesthetics*, 12.
5 M. H. Abrams, *The Mirror and the Lamp: Romantic Theory and the Critical Tradition* (Oxford: Oxford University Press, 1953). Partly in contrast to Abrams's expressivist model of Romanticism, some critics have emphasized the continuities between Enlightenment and Romanticism – for example, Philippe Lacoue-Labarthe and Jean-Luc Nancy, *The Literary Absolute: The Theory of Literature in German Romanticism* (Albany: State University of New York Press, 1988); Marshall Brown, 'Romanticism and Enlightenment', in *The Cambridge Companion to British Romanticism* (Cambridge: Cambridge University Press, 1993) and *The Cambridge History of Literary Criticism, Vol. V: Romanticism* (Cambridge: Cambridge University Press, 2000); and Charles LeBlanc et al., *La forme poétique du monde. Anthologie du romantisme allemand* (Paris: José Corti, 2003).
6 See Mario Praz, *The Romantic Agony* (Oxford: Oxford University Press, 1970).
7 Abrams, *The Mirror and the Lamp*, 22. Italics are mine.
8 M.H. Abrams, 'Theories of (Western) Poetry', in *The New Princeton Encyclopedia of Poetry and Poetics* (Princeton: Princeton University Press, 1993), 643.
9 Novalis in W.H. Auden, *The Enchafèd Flood: Or the Romantic Iconography of the Sea* (London: Forgotten Books, 2015), 58.
10 Honour, *Romanticism*, 18.
11 Immanuel Kant, *Critique of the Power of Judgment* (New York: Cambridge University Press, 2000), paragraphs 46–50.
12 For Kant, a genius is someone who has the talent to receive the rules of nature without knowing these rules and while being ignorant of how they have employed them. Following this definition, Newton is a great mind but not a genius, because he was able to explain, both to himself and to others, how he came to his discoveries. Contrary to that of the artist, Newton's discovery can be followed and imitated.

13 David Punter, 'Romanticism', in Martin Coyle et al. (eds), *Encyclopedia of Literature and Criticism* (New York: Routledge, 2003 [1991]), 107. My emphasis.
14 See Nathalie Heinich, *The Glory of Van Gogh: An Anthropology of Admiration* (Princeton: Princeton University Press, 1996) and *Être écrivain. Création et identité* (Paris: Découverte, 2000).
15 Friedrich Schlegel, *Athenaeum* Fragment 415, in *Friedrich Schlegel's Lucinde and the Fragments* (Minneapolis: University of Minnesota Press, 1971).
16 Schlegel, *Athenaeum* Fragment 116.
17 Schlegel, *Ideas* Fragment 44. Italics are mine.
18 Schiller, 'Über Bürgers Gedichte'. Cited from Martha Woodmansee, *The Author, Art, and the Market* (New York: Columbia University Press, 1996), 115. Italics are mine.
19 William Wordsworth, 'Advertisement to *Lyrical Ballads* (1798)', in *Prose Works of William Wordsworth* (Oxford: Clarendon Press, 1974), 126.
20 Lacoue-Labarthe and Nancy, *The Literary Absolute*, 48–9.
21 Schlegel, *Ideas* Fragment 64.
22 Although many scholars count Schiller among the Romantics (e.g. LeBlanc et al. 2003), he is just as often counted among the German idealists (e.g. Rüdiger Safranski, *Schiller oder die Erfindung des deutchen Idealismus*. Munich: Carl Hanser Verlag, 2004). Nevertheless, all agree that Schiller's letters on the aesthetic education of man are to be conceived of as the impetus of Romantic thought. Overall, there is a lot of disagreement as to who are exactly to be counted among the German Romantics and who among the German Idealists. Schelling, for instance, is taken by most scholars to be an idealist (e.g. by LeBlanc et al., *La forme poétique du monde*; and Martin Heidegger, *Schelling's Treatise on the Essence of Freedom*. Ohio: Ohio University Press, 1985 [1809]), but plays a key role in Lacoue-Labarthe's and Nancy's book on German Romanticism (Lacoue-Labarthe and Nancy, *The Literary Absolute*). The same goes for Fichte, who is counted by Heidegger among the idealists (Martin Heidegger, *Der Deutsche Idealismus (Fichte,*

Hegel, Schelling) und die philosophische Problemlage der Gegenwart. Frankfurt a/M: Vittorio Klostermann, 1997), but treated by Lacoue-Labarthe and Nancy as the father of Romanticism and by both LeBlanc et al. and Frank (Manfred Frank, *The Philosophical Foundations of Early German Romanticism*. New York: State University of New York Press, 2004) even as one of the most important Romantics. Hölderlin, for his part, is considered a Romantic by most scholars, but is, according to others, a severe critic of Romanticism (e.g. Jean-Luc Nancy, 'The Poet's Calculation', in *Expectation: Philosophy, Literature*. New York: Fordham University Press, 2018, 83–107; Philippe Lacoue-Labarthe, *Heidegger and the Politics of Poetry*. Urbana: University of Illinois Press, 2007). There is complete unanimity only with regard to the Schlegel brothers: their *Athenaeum* journal can safely be regarded as the heart of German Romanticism.

23 'This great action, because of its tenor and its consequences, touches everyone who calls himself a man, so, because of its method of procedure, it must especially interest every independent thinker.' Friedrich Schiller, *On the Aesthetic Education of Man* (New York: Dover Publications, 2004), 26.

24 Schiller, *On the Aesthetic Education of Man*, 29.

25 Ibid., 30.

26 Immanuel Kant, *An Answer to the Question: What is Enlightenment?* (Cambridge: Cambridge University Press, 1991 [1784]).

27 Schiller, *On the Aesthetic Education of Man*, 40.

28 Ibid., 46.

29 Ibid., 60. Note that Schiller speaks of the 'person' instead of the 'individual'. That is, he uses the notion of the individual in the usual sense of the word and reserves the notion of the 'person' for what I call 'individual' in this chapter. Significant in this respect is the following remark in one of Schiller's last letters: 'Ignorant of his *own* human dignity, he [who is led by his passions, AvR] is far removed from honoring it in others, and conscious of his own savage greed, he fears it in every creature that resembles him. He never perceives others

in himself, only himself in others; and society, instead of expanding him into the species, only confines him ever more closely inside his individuality.' Schiller, *On the Aesthetic Education of Man*, 114.

30 Ibid., 62.
31 Ibid., 64.
32 Ibid., 73.
33 Ibid., 97.
34 Schiller anticipates this dominant reception by claiming that 'there is a fine *art of passion*, but an impassioned fine *art* is a contradiction in terms, for the inevitable effect of the *Beautiful* is freedom from passions.' Schiller, *On the Aesthetic Education of Man*, 106–7.
35 Ibid., 86.
36 To be more precise, Karl Philip Moritz was the first to develop the idea of aesthetic autonomy in his essay 'Versuch einer Vereinigung aller schönen Künste und Wissenschaften unter dem Begriff des in sichselbst Vollendeten (1785)', in *Schriften zur Ästhetik und Poetik* (Tübingen: H.J. Schrimpf, 1962). Kant follows Moritz in this respect. See also Woodmansee, *The Author, Art, and the Market*.
37 Kant, *Critique of the Power of Judgment*, paragraph 58. Italics are mine.
38 Loesberg's *A Return to Aesthetics* is, to a large extent, devoted to eliminating the source of this misunderstanding.
39 Schlegel, *Athenaeum* Fragment 3.
40 Schlegel, *Critical* Fragment 80. Italics are mine. In the above-cited fragment 116, Schlegel also associates poetry with 'in-betweenness': 'poetry which can best glide *between* the portrayer and what is portrayed ... [o]n the wings of poetic reflection'.
41 See also Schlegel, *Athenaeum* Fragment 22.
42 Schlegel, *Athenaeum* Fragment 206. Translation slightly modified. The English translation speaks of a 'porcupine', but hedgehog is closer to the German original *Igel*.
43 Alluding to Lacoue-Labarthe and Nancy in *The Literary Absolute*, 43–4: 'To write the fragment is to write fragments.' With regard to the early Romanticist's relation with the Absolute, see also Maurice Blanchot,

The Infinite Conversation (Minneapolis: University of Minnesota Press, 1993).

44 Schlegel, *Athenaeum* Fragment 121.
45 Schlegel, *Ideas* Fragment 95. Schlegel does, however, compare all-encompassing romantic poetry with the Bible. To quote the fragment 95 in its entirety: 'The new, eternal gospel that Lessing prophesied would appear as a bible: but not as a single book in the usual sense. Even what we now call the Bible is in fact a system of books. And that is, I might add, no mere arbitrary turn of phrase! Or is there some other word to differentiate the idea of an infinite book from an ordinary one, rather than Bible, the book per se, the absolute book? And surely there is an eternally essential and even practical difference if a book is merely a means to an end, or an independent work, an individual, a personified idea. It cannot be this without divine inspiration, and here the esoteric concept is itself in agreement with the exoteric one; and, moreover, no idea is isolated, but is what it is only in combination with all other ideas. An example will explain this. All the classical poems of the ancients are coherent, inseparable; they form an organic whole, they constitute, properly viewed, only a single poem, the only one in which poetry itself appears in perfection. In a similar way, in a perfect literature, all books should be only a single book and, as such, in an eternally developing book, the gospel of humanity and culture will be revealed.'
46 Schlegel, *Athenaeum* Fragment 242.
47 Schiller, *On the Aesthetic Education of Man*, 40.
48 In this respect, the German Romantics often refer to the 'chemical' nature of poetry. See, for instance, Schlegel, *Critical* Fragment 34: 'A witty idea is a disintegration of spiritual substances which, before being suddenly separated, must have been thoroughly mixed. The imagination must first be satiated with all sorts of life before one can electrify it with the friction of free social intercourse so that the slightest friendly or hostile touch can elicit brilliant sparks and lustrous rays – or smashing thunderbolts.' Similarly, the Romantics characterize their poetic activities as an experimental chemical combination called *sympoetry*.

49 Novalis, quoted from *Novalis: Notes for a Romantic Encyclopaedia. Das Algemeine Brouillon*, ed. David W. Wood (New York: State University of New York Press, 2007), xvi.
50 Schiller, *On the Aesthetic Education of Man*, 138.
51 First of all, that of the dualism of autonomy and heteronomy. Because, as we have seen, the Romantics tried to overcome the opposition between autonomy and heteronomy, among other things, by avoiding these terms, Rancière's description of Romanticism's original scene as an emplotment of autonomy and heteronomy is somewhat misleading. For a more extensive analysis of the Romanticist attitude vis à vis Kantian dualism, see Vinod Lakshmipathy, 'Kant and the Turn to Romanticism', *Kritike* 3.2 (2009): 90–102. Lakshmipathy's main thesis can be summarized as follows: 'For the Romantics like Schelling, even though Kant had taken the essential steps to indicate the finitude of human reason, and therefore had made progress in resolving the long-drawn-out dispute between dogmatism and scepticism, the vestiges of these steps appeared as the non-desirable presence of dualisms in the Kantian system. For the Romantics, it is precisely these dualisms that render the Kantian system incomplete. Their complaint was that Kant could never satisfactorily explain the interaction between the domains, noumena and the phenomena, which suggested an impasse in the Kantian system.' (91)
52 In a way, 'autonomy' has become synonymous with 'absolute' (*ab* = away from; *solver* = loosen).
53 These quotes are all taken from Felski's *Uses of Literature*, but similar ones can easily be found in other anti-autonomist works.
54 This is, of course, an expression of the eighteenth- and nineteenth-century ideal of intellectual emancipation. A wonderful illustration of this ideal can be found in Jacques Rancière's *The Ignorant Schoolmaster: Five Lessons on Intellectual Emancipation* (Stanford: Stanford University Press, 1991). Rancière describes the pedagogical practice of Joseph Jacotot, a Francophone teacher of French at the Flemish University of Leuven, in the year 1818. Because he himself does not speak Dutch, Jacotot decides not to teach his Dutch-speaking students, but to have them teach themselves by studying a bilingual novel. While his students

learn French, he himself is just as much a student learning Dutch. At the basis of this educational practice is the premise of equal intelligence of master and student.

55 Of course, a perversion of this idea in the form of prescriptive cultural politics is quite easy, as has been emphasized in many literary historical studies. What I wished to highlight in this chapter is that such a perversion can only be considered *intrinsic* to the idea of literary autonomy when autonomy is indeed conceived of as a form of social withdrawal.

56 This will be dealt with briefly in the next chapter. For a more extensive overview of the Anglo-Saxon reception of Kant and German Romanticism, see, for instance, the chapter 'Organic Form: From New Criticism to Coleridge and Kant', in Loesberg's *A Return to Aesthetics*.

Chapter 2

1 For an overview of nineteenth- and twentieth-century thought about the subject, see Charles Taylor, *Sources of the Self: The Making of Modern Identity* (Cambridge, MA: Harvard University Press, 1989); Philippe Lacoue-Labarthe, *The Subject of Philosophy* (Minneapolis: University of Minnesota Press, 1993); Donald E. Hall, *Subjectivity* (New York: Routledge, 2004); Jerrold Seigel, *The Idea of the Self: Thought and Experience in Western Europe since the Seventeenth Century* (Cambridge: Cambridge University Press, 2005); Alberto Toscano, *The Theatre of Production: Philosophy and Individuation from Kant to Deleuze* (London: Palgrave Macmillan, 2006); and Josef Früchtl, *The Impertinent Self: A Heroic History of Modernity* (Stanford: Stanford University Press, 2009).

2 Charles Taylor, *Hegel* (Cambridge: Cambridge University Press, 1975), 561.

3 Friedrich Nietzsche, *The Birth of Tragedy Out of the Spirit of Music* (Oxford: Oxford University Press, 2008).

4 Hall, *Subjectivity*, 71.

5   Paul Ricoeur, *Freud and Philosophy: An Essay on Interpretation* (London: Yale University Press, 1970).
6   This is why Früchtl, in his book on the history of modernity, concludes: 'Alongside dialecticians, deconstructivists, and genealogists trained in psychology or sociology, we have to evaluate the idea that there is one single thing that owes its existence entirely to self-determination ... untouched by negative detrimental conditions as an *illusion*.' Früchtl, *The Impertinent Self*, 131.
7   Although the later Foucault in a way returns to this view, albeit indirectly through a reading of Ancient philosophy concerning the care for the self.
8   Michel Foucault, *The Order of Things: An Archeology of the Human Sciences* (London: Routledge, 2004 [1970]), 422.
9   See also Toscano, *The Theatre of Production*, 60.
10 See also Donald Walhout, 'The Hermeneutical Turn in American Critical Theory, 1830–1860', *Journal of the History of Ideas* 57.4 (1996): 683–703.
11 Taylor, *Sources of the Self*, 420.
12 Friedrich Schleiermacher, *Hermeneutics and Criticism, and Other Writings* (Cambridge: Cambridge University Press, 1998), 23.
13 Friedrich Schlegel, *Dialogue on Poetry and Literary Aphorisms* (Pennsylvania: Pennsylvania State University Press, 1968).
14 Safranski, *Romanticism*. See also Friedrich Schlegel, 'On Incomprehensibility', in *Friedrich Schlegel's Lucinde and the Fragments*.
15 Martin Heidegger, *Elucidations of Hölderlin's Poetry* (Amherst, NY: Humanities Books, 2000). Apart from Heidegger, Gadamer as well can be conceived of as a late heir to the hermeneutic turn. In *The Relevance of Beauty*, Gadamer stresses that modern art can best be understood as a *play* that derives its meaning from the moment it plays itself rather than from the play's outcome. Hans-Georg Gadamer, *The Relevance of Beauty, and Other Essays* (Cambridge: Cambridge University Press, 1986).
16 See also Gayle Ormiston and Alan Schrift (eds), *Transforming the Hermeneutic Context: From Nietzsche to Nancy* (New York: SUNY Press, 1989). The hermeneutic turn is somewhat hidden from sight,

because after Romanticism, many writers, artists and critics keep on describing literary practice in terms of truth. A telling example is the twentieth-century avant-garde movements. Truth, though, even in these movements, is conceived of as something that is concealed, something that has to be created or that can only be caught in a glimpse. It is this kind of problematization of a manifest truth that is an indication of the hermeneutic turn.

17 Jacques Rancière, 'The Aesthetic Revolution and Its Outcomes: Emplotments of Autonomy and Heteronomy', *New Left Review* 14 (2002): 135.
18 Schiller, *On the Aesthetic Education of Man*, 80. Italics are mine.
19 Rancière, 'The Aesthetic Revolution and Its Outcomes', 133. This essay has been republished in Jacques Rancière, *Dissensus: On Politics and Aesthetics* (London/New York: Continuum, 2010).
20 Loesberg, *A Return to Aesthetics*, 99.
21 Rancière, 'The Aesthetic Revolution and Its Outcomes', 134.
22 This is why the romantic paradigm is indeed a *paradigm* – including not only aesthetics, but also an anthropology, sociology and politics.
23 Bennett, 'Sociology, Aesthetics, Expertise', 165. Italics are mine.
24 This was not a mere pragmatic solution. After the catastrophes of European fascism and national-socialism, every form of aestheticization of politics or politicization of aesthetics had a suspicious ring.
25 Hans Ulrich Gumbrecht, *Atmosphere, Mood, Stimmung: On a Hidden Potential of Literature* (Stanford: Stanford University Press, 2012), 3.
26 For a more elaborate analysis of this debate, see Albert Cassange, *Théorie de l'art pour l'art chez les derniers romantiques et les premiers réalistes* (Seyssel: Editions Champ Vallon, 1906).
27 Cassange, *Théorie de l'art pour l'art*, 140. Translations are mine. After having enumerated the misleading associations that over the years have stuck to the catchy slogan of art for art's sake – elitism, self-reference, subjectivism, incommunicability and so on – Cassange concludes that 'one really has to know very little of Romanticism to adopt a thesis like this.' (72)
28 Cassange, *Théorie de l'art pour l'art*, 74.

29 Ibid.
30 Daniel Oster, 'Préface', in *Théorie de l'art pour l'art*, 19. A quite similar thesis can be found in Goldstone, *Fictions of Autonomy*, 5: 'My approach treats the aestheticists' practices of modernism *as* its social program. I show that it is by pursuing relative autonomy as a *mode of relation* between literature and the social world of its emergence that modernism's engagements with its contexts comes about.'
31 See, for example, Safranski, *Romanticism*, chapters 10 and 11.
32 See Frans Ruiter and Wilbert Smulders, *Literatuur en moderniteit in Nederland, 1840–1990* [Literature and Modernity in the Netherlands, 1840–1990] (Amsterdam/Antwerp: Arbeiderspers, 1996), especially Chapter 6.
33 See Oster, 'Préface'.
34 Or, as Terry Eagleton has it in *The Ideology of the Aesthetic*: 'The construction of the modern notion of the aesthetic artifact is thus inseparable from the construction of the dominant ideological forms of modern class society and indeed from a whole new form of human subjectivity appropriate to that social order. It is on this account, rather than because men and women have suddenly awoken to the supreme value of painting or poetry, that aesthetics plays so obtrusive a role in the intellectual heritage of the present.' Terry Eagleton, *The Ideology of the Aesthetic* (Oxford: Blackwell, 1990), 3. It is not necessary to adopt a neo-Marxist perspective to see that nineteenth- and twentieth-century literary debates lead to this conclusion.
35 Ferdinand Tönnies, *Community and Civil Society* (Cambridge: Cambridge University Press, 2001 [1979]).
36 Früchtl, *The Impertinent Self*, 135–6.
37 Eagleton, *The Ideology of the Aesthetic*, 25.
38 Jacques Rancière, 'The Shortcomings of the Notion of Modernity', in *The Politics of Aesthetics*.
39 Rancière, *The Politics of Aesthetics*, 21. The thesis that the notion of modernity does not refer to a well-defined historical period, but is rather the indication of a fundamental tension that reverts back to Romantic ambiguity, can also be found with other scholars.

40 Rancière, *The Politics of Aesthetics*, 21.
41 For a more elaborate analysis of the influence and reception of M.H. Abrams's work, see Aukje van Rooden, 'Magnifying *The Mirror and the Lamp*: A Critical Reconsideration of the Abramsian Poetical Model and Its Contribution to the Research of Modern Dutch Literature', *Journal of Dutch Literature* 3.1 (2012): 65–87.
42 Abrams, *The Mirror and the Lamp*, 6.
43 Abrams, 'Theories of (Western) Poetry', 639. Italics are mine.
44 Abrams, *The Mirror and the Lamp*, 326–7.
45 Loesberg, *A Return to Aesthetics*, 25.
46 For a more elaborate analysis of Coleridge's influence on New Criticism, see, for example, Cleanth Brooks, 'Implications of an Organic Theory of Poetry', in M.H. Abrams (ed.), *Literature and Belief: English Institute Essays* (New York: Columbia University Press, 1957). For a more elaborate analysis of Coleridge's relation to Kant and German Romanticism, see the chapter 'Organic Form', in Loesberg's *A Return to Aesthetics*. Loesberg is not the only one emphasizing the remarkable reception of German Romanticism by Coleridge. For an overview of studies that have investigated Coleridge's reception of German Romanticism, see Loesberg, *A Return to Aesthetics*, 241 and note 9.
47 Although the sociological, institutional and contextual turns in literary studies were presented and experienced as a necessary turning away from the hermetically studied text towards the context, they are, in their affirmation of the gap between the two, a reinforcement, of course, of the autonomist approach to literature.
48 A case in point is the 2011 special issue *Context?* of the *New Literary History*. Among its contributors are Rita Felski, Martin Jay, Derek Attridge and Claire Colebrook. The overall aim of this special issue is to question the distinction between text and context. 'Context?', *New Literary History* 42.4 (2011).
49 Goldstone, *Fictions of Autonomy*, 4.
50 Jusdanis, *Fiction Agonistes*, 3.
51 Stinson, *Satirizing Modernism*, 6 and 47.

52 If we take one step back, three phases can be discerned in this gradual process. Each phase represents a different stance towards modernity, embracing different shared premises and choosing different points of attack. The first phase can be called the *bourgeois* phase and starts from the early nineteenth century. The shared premise during this phase is the premise that literature is able to reform and elevate society. The area of debate is whether or not this literature should be autonomous. The second phase can be called the *modern* phase and starts in the mid-nineteenth century. The shared premise during this second phase is the premise that literature is a product of its age and thus embedded in its own time. The area of debate during this phase is the question as to what extent literature that is a product of its age can still reform and elevate society. The third phase can be called the *post-modern* phase and starts in the mid-twentieth century. The shared premise during this phase is the premise that the grand narratives of societal reform and elevation have lost their persuasiveness. The area of debate during this phase is the question as to what extent literature can still have a social, moral or political dimension.
53 Toscano, *The Theatre of Production*, 2.
54 Rudolphe Gasché, *Of Minimal Things: Studies on the Notion of Relation* (Stanford: Stanford University Press, 1999). To be honest, Gasché does not speak of autonomy and heteronomy, but of the 'non relational' and the 'relational'. Alberto Toscano, too, situates the possibility of a true conception of relationality in the twentieth century, albeit not so much in the work of Heidegger as Gasché does, but in that of Simondon and Deleuze: 'This intervention [of the organic, AvR], prefigured in various strands of post-Kantian philosophy, from Schelling to Peirce, but only truly carried out in the works of Gilbert Simondon and Gilles Deleuze, will radically transfigure the presuppositions and results of critique and of its concept of the transcendental, by conferring full rights upon that genetic modality of individuation which is only problematically inscribed in Kant's own writings ... specifically, with the formulation of a distinction between autonomy and heteronomy as Kant's provisional and problematic response to this question'. Toscano, *The Theatre of Production*, 2.

Chapter 3

1 Theodor W. Adorno and Max Horkheimer, *Dialectic of Enlightenment* (New York: Verso, 1997), 135.
2 Jusdanis, *Fiction Agonistes*, 3. See also page 4: 'A paradox wends through my study, namely that literature is autonomous and simultaneously socially embedded.'
3 See also Adorno, *Aesthetic Theory*, 309: 'What is social in art is its immanent movement against society, not its manifest opinions.'
4 Jacques Rancière, *Aisthesis: Scenes from the Aesthetic Regime of Art* (New York: Verso Books, 2013), x. Italics are mine.
5 Rancière is describing the interruption of what he calls the 'representative regime' by the 'aesthetic regime'. See Jacques Rancière in particular, *Mute Speech: Literature, Critical Theory and Politics* (New York: Columbia University Press, 2011) and *The Politics of Literature* (Cambridge: Polity Press, 2011).
6 As Rancière has it in *The Future of the Image*: 'To see something as art … means seeing two things at once. … It works in the first instance towards the construction of a new visibility. A new form of painting [or literature, AvR] is one that offers itself to eyes that are trained to see differently'. Jacques Rancière, *The Future of the Image* (New York: Verso Books, 2007), 81. A similar argument is developed by Adorno in his *Aesthetic Theory*, which distinguishes between forms of audibility: 'This double character [of art, AvR] becomes physiognomically decipherable, whether intentionally so or not, when one views or listens to art from an external vantage point, and, certainly, art always stands in need of this external perspective for protection from the fetishization of its autonomy. Music, whether it is played in a café or, as is often the case in America, piped into restaurants, can be transformed into something completely different, of which the hum of conversation and the rattle of dishes and whatever else becomes a part. … Yet someone sitting in a café who is suddenly struck by the music and listens intensely may feel odd to himself and seem foolish to others. In

this antagonism, the fundamental relation of art and society appears. The continuity of art is destroyed when it is experienced externally, just as medleys willfully destroy it in the material.' Adorno, *Aesthetic Theory*, 342–3.

7   Rancière, *The Future of the Image*, 121.
8   For a similar evaluation of Rancière's aesthetics, see Bennett, 'Sociology, Aesthetics, Expertise', 164: 'The key limitation of Rancière's position in this regard is that his historicization of aesthetics stops short at Kant, whose *Critique of [the Power of, AvR] Judgment* he sees as the crucial foundational event establishing the aesthetic regime of art.'
9   Indeed, both Adorno and Rancière are followers of Marx, one of the three 'masters of suspicion' who, according to the earlier quoted phrase of Donald E. Hall, are but 'another nineteenth-century manifestation of a quasi-self-help philosophy'. Hall, *Subjectivity*, 71.
10 See George Dickie, *Art and the Aesthetic: An Institutional Analysis* (New York: Cornell University Press, 1974); and Pierre Bourdieu, *Distinction: A Social Critique on the Judgment of Taste* (New York: Routledge, 1984).
11 Arthur Danto, 'The Artworld', *Journal of Philosophy* 61 (1964): 571–84. The notion of the 'open concept' originally stems from Morris Weitz, 'The Role of Theory in Aesthetics', *JAAC* 15 (1956): 27–35. For a more extensive analysis of the sociological relational turn, see Alex Neill and Aaron Ridley, 'Relational Theories of Art: The History of an Error', *British Journal of Aesthetics* 52.2 (2012): 141–51.
12 See, for example, Shira Wolosky, 'Relational Aesthetics and Feminist Poetics', *New Literary History* 41.3 (2010): 571–91. For a more general analysis, see also Eagleton's *The Ideology of the Aesthetic*.
13 Seigel, *The Idea of the Self*, 5.
14 Another way of putting this is, as Tony Bennett has it, to say that the social is 'relocated' on the most fundamental level. Bennett is one of the very few literary theorists conceiving literature's social dimension to be relational in this fundamental sense of the word. His attempt to 'relocate the social' is an interesting impetus to the relational paradigm developed here. Bennett, 'Sociology, Aesthetics, Expertise'.

15 This relationality resonates with developments in a variety of disciplines concerning *agencement* (Gilles Deleuze and Claire Parnet, *Dialogues*. London: The Athlone Press, 1987; Manuel De Landa, *A New Philosophy of Society: Assemblage Theory and Social Complexity*. New York: Continuum, 2006) and *agency* (Catriona Mackenzie and Nataliw Stoljar (eds), *Relational Autonomy: Feminist Perspectives on Autonomy, Agency and the Social Self*. New York: Oxford University Press, 2000), as well as insights in the fields of contemporary sociology (Michael Hardt and Antonio Negri, *Common Wealth*. Harvard: Belknap Press, 2009; Bruno Latour, *Reassembling the Social: An Introduction to Actor-Network-Theory*. Oxford: Oxford University Press, 2005), contemporary theories on (postcolonial) language and literature (Éduard Glissant, *Poetics of Relation*. Ann Arbor: University of Michigan Press, 1997; Hans Ulrich Gumbrecht, *Atmosphere, Mood, Stimmung: On a Hidden Potential of Literature*. Stanford: Stanford University Press, 2012; and Caroline Levine, *Forms: Whole, Rhythm, Hierarchy, Network*. Princeton: Princeton University Press, 2015), and neurobiology (Francisco Varela, Evan Thompson and Eleanor Rosch, *The Embodied Mind: Cognitive Science and Human Experience*. Cambridge: MIT Press, 1991).
Hans Ulrich Gumbrecht makes a promising case for understanding literature's 'hidden potential' in terms of Heidegger's existential notion of *Stimmung*, but in the end he, too, succumbs to a form of contextualism. Literature's mood appears, for Gumbrecht, not to be the way in which a literary work exists, but the spirit of the times at the moment of its conception. The relationality developed in *Atmosphere, Mood, Stimmung* is therefore not an ontological one, but a hermeneutic form of relationality that demands of the reader the deciphering of the author's horizon of understanding. Similarly promising is Caroline Levine's redefinition of form, which could be read as a formalist account of the relational paradigm. In the end, however, Levine seems to resort to a *conjunction* of a primarily separated text and context that is very similar to the Romantic conjunction of art and life, arguing 'that forms organize *not only* works of art *but also* political life'. Levine, *Forms*, back flap.

16 Jacques Rancière, *The Emancipated Spectator* (New York: Verso Books, 2009).

17 See Nicolas Bourriaud, *Formes de vie: L'art moderne et l'invention de soi* (Paris: Denoël, 1999), *Postproduction: Culture as Screenplay: How Art Reprogrammes the World* (New York: Lukas & Sternberg, 2005) and *The Radicant* (New York: Sternberg, 2009).

18 Nicolas Bourriaud, 'Precarious Constructions: Answer to Jacques Rancière on Art and Politics', *Open* 17 (2009): 1–8.

19 Nicolas Bourriaud, *Relational Aesthetics* (Dijon: Les Presses du Réel, 2002), 21.

20 Bourriaud, 'Precarious Constructions'.

21 In his analysis of 'community art', Pascal Gielen also aims to expand Bourriaud's relational aesthetics to an aesthetics encompassing all forms of art. In so doing, he develops a rather complicated cartography of 'auto-relational', 'allo-relational', 'digestive' and 'subversive' art forms which is not only quite essentialist in nature, but also ends up affirming the distinction between autonomy and heteronomy that it proposed to overcome. Pascal Gielen, 'Mapping Community Art', in Paul De Bruyne and Pascal Gielen (eds), *Community Art: The Politics of Trespassing* (Amsterdam: Valiz, 2011).

22 For introductions into the work of Nancy, see, for instance, Ian James, *The Fragmentary Demand: An Introduction to the Philosophy of Jean-Luc Nancy* (Stanford: Stanford University Press, 2006); and Marie-Eve Morin, *Jean-Luc Nancy* (Cambridge: Polity Press, 2012). Recently, a large number of Nancy's texts on literature have been collected in one volume. See Jean-Luc Nancy, *Expectation: Philosophy, Literature* (New York: Fordham University Press, 2018).

23 See Jean-Luc Nancy, *The Sense of the World* (Minneapolis: University of Minnesota Press, 1998), *Being Singular Plural* (Stanford: Stanford University Press, 2000) and *The Creation of the World, or Globalization* (Albany: State University of New York Press, 2007). In these works, Nancy radicalizes Heidegger's analysis of being-there (*Dasein*). Even though he follows Heidegger to a very large extent, Nancy reproaches him for not having taken the being-with (*Mitsein*) of being-there

(*Dasein*) seriously enough. According to Nancy, being-with is not a qualification of being-there, as though being-there can somehow exist without existing *with* others. Being-with is rather the way in which being-there constitutes itself. For an extensive analysis of Nancy on the being-with, see Ignaas Devisch, *Jean-Luc Nancy and the Question of Community* (New York: Bloomsbury, 2012).

24 Jean-Luc Nancy, *The Experience of Freedom* (Stanford: Stanford University Press, 1993), 69.
25 Nancy, *Being Singular Plural*, 57–8.
26 Ibid., 57–8.
27 Novalis, quoted from *Novalis: Notes for a Romantic Encyclopaedia*, xvi.
28 Jean-Luc Nancy, *The Inoperative Community* (Minneapolis: University of Minnesota Press, 1991), 25–6. Italics are mine.
29 This view of literature as a praxis of sharing not only echoes Bourriaud's view of participatory art but also a number of recent reflections on what is generally called 'the common'. In brief, the common is a form of community that keeps the mid-way between the nineteenth-century ideal of the autonomous individual and the twentieth-century ideal of a fusion of individuals to create some form of political collective.
30 Nancy, *The Creation of the World*, 53.
31 As we have seen, the German Romantics, too, were seeking the social relevance of literature in this form of 'realism'. Contrary to the German Idealists, the Romantics believed literature to be the instant realization of human freedom and morality instead of its prefiguration (or symbol, in the Kantian sense of the word). In this respect, too, the relational paradigm is thus a continuation of the Romantic paradigm.
32 Loesberg, *A Return to Aesthetics*, 98. Italics are mine.
33 Thierry De Duve, *Kant after Duchamp* (Cambridge: MIT Press, 1998), 357.
34 Jacques Derrida, 'Passions: An Oblique Offering', in *On the Name* (Stanford: Stanford University Press, 1995), 28. Translation slightly modified.
35 Rancière, *Aisthesis*, x. Italics are mine.

36 This idea of the absolute freedom of modern literature is, of course, not unrelated to the 'anything goes' often critically attributed to so-called purely aesthetic, non-committal literature. In what follows, I hope to show that one can also value it more positively as implying the social relevance of literature.
37 '"Art" is everything that is called art. Far from being a sophism, it constitutes the ontological specificity of works of art.' De Duve, *Kant after Duchamp*, 12.
38 De Duve, *Kant after Duchamp*, 13. Italics are mine.
39 Maurice Blanchot, *The Work of Fire* (Stanford: Stanford University Press, 1995), 315–6. Translation slightly modified.
40 Blanchot, *The Work of Fire*, 301–2.
41 This is, in a nutshell, Sartre's view on literary *engagement*. In a crucial passage in *What Is Literature?* he claims: 'Kant believes that the work of art first exists as fact and that it is then seen. Whereas it exists only if one *looks* at it and if it is first pure appeal, pure exigence to exist. It is not an instrument whose existence is manifest and whose end is undetermined. It presents itself as a task to be discharged; from the very beginning it places itself on the level of the categorical imperative. You are perfectly free to leave that book on the table. But if you open it, you assume responsibility for it.' Jean Paul Sartre, *'What Is Literature?' and Other Essays* (Cambridge, MA: Harvard University Press, 1988), 56.
42 Richard Rorty, *Contingency, Irony, and Solidarity* (Cambridge: Cambridge University Press, 1989), 3.
43 Rorty bases himself on Judith Shklar's definition of liberals as 'the people who think that cruelty is the worst thing we do' (Rorty, *Contingency, Irony, and Solidarity*, xv and 74). For Shklar, see *Ordinary Vices* (1984). It is remarkable that a definition which plays such a central role in his argumentation is subscribed to by Rorty without further explanation or analysis.
44 Those who succeed in doing so are called 'liberal ironists' by Rorty.
45 Rorty, *Contingency, Irony, and Solidarity*, xvi. Italics are mine.
46 Ibid., 107. Italics are mine.
47 Ibid., 142.

48 It is very doubtful whether this is so evident. Where 'the ability to *feel* pain' could perhaps be seen as a universal ability that transcends the contingency of different social discourses, as Rorty claims (Rorty, *Contingency, Irony, and Solidarity*, 88. Italics are mine), the *recognition* and *acknowledgement* of pain needed for solidarity do not seem to be universal at all. Although slaves were undeniably capable of feeling pain, this pain was not always recognized and acknowledged as such. The same holds true for the suffering of animals in the widely accepted practice of factory farming. The ability to recognize the suffering of others seems, in other words, still determined by the contingent language game of a certain historical period. Instead of developing a sensitivity to the suffering of others, developing a sensitivity to *contingency itself* seems to me, therefore, the ultimate aim of (liberal) democracy – which is indeed, as we shall see, the ethical value central to the relational paradigm.
49 Rorty, *Contingency, Irony, and Solidarity*, 141. In Rorty's case, the dividing line between the two types of novels is therefore parallel to the dividing line between the private and the public: 'The public-private distinction I developed throughout Part II suggests that we distinguish books which help us to become autonomous from books that help us to become less cruel' (Rorty, *Contingency, Irony, and Solidarity*, 141). Rorty's view on literature has been criticized from various angles. See Robert Brandom (ed.), *Rorty and His Critics* (Oxford: Blackwell Publishing, 2000). Most of the criticism concerns Rorty's strict separation between the public and the private, and the related classification of types of novels.
50 Rorty, *Contingency, Irony, and Solidarity*, 141.
51 Ibid.
52 Milan Kundera, *The Art of the Novel* (New York: HarperCollins, 1986); Todorov, *La littérature en péril*; and Martha Nussbaum, *Love's Knowledge: Essays on Philosophy and Literature* (Oxford: Oxford University Press, 1992). It should be noted that those associated with the so-called 'ethical turn' in literary theory often look for a productive tension between both categories. Nevertheless, this is once again an

attempt to *bridge* the dualism of modernity rather than an attempt to overcome it.

53 Rorty, *Contingency, Irony, and Solidarity*, 142.
54 Maurice Blanchot, *The Space of Literature* (Lincoln: University of Nebraska Press, 1982), 228. See also page 75.
55 Blanchot, *The Work of Fire*, 315–6.
56 Jean-Luc Nancy, *The Muses* (Stanford: Stanford University Press, 1996), 76.
57 See also Nancy, *Being Singular Plural*, 11.
58 In Casanova's *The World Republic of Letters*, both trends are combined. Pascale Casanova, *The World Republic of Letters* (Cambridge, MA: Harvard University Press, 2004).
59 Thierry De Duve, 'Art Was a Proper Name', in *Kant after Duchamp*, especially 52.
60 Respectively Todorov, *La littérature en péril*; Bourdieu, *Firing Back 2*; Jusdanis, *Fiction Agonistes*; Loesberg, *A Return to Aesthetics*; and Felski, *Uses of Literature*.

Bibliography

Abrams, Meier Howard (1953), *The Mirror and the Lamp: Romantic Theory and the Critical Tradition*. New York: Oxford University Press.

Abrams, Meier Howard (1993), 'Theories of (Western) Poetry', in *The New Princeton Encyclopedia of Poetry and Poetics*. Princeton: Princeton University Press, 639–49.

Adorno, Theodor W. (1992), 'Commitment', in *Notes to Literature*, vol. 2. New York: Columbia University Press. Translation of 'Engagement oder die künslerische Autonomie', in *Die neue Rundschau* 73:1, 1962.

Adorno, Theodor W. (1997), *Aesthetic Theory*. New York: Bloomsbury. Translation of *Ästhetische Theorie: Gesammelte Schriften 7*. Frankfurt a/M: Suhrkamp, 1970.

Adorno, Theodor W. and Max Horkheimer (1997), *Dialectic of Enlightenment*. New York: Verso. Translation of *Dialektik der Aufklärung*, 1944.

Alphen, Ernst van, Mieke Bal and Carel E. Smith (2009), *The Rhetoric of Sincerity*. Stanford: Stanford University Press.

Altes, Liesbeth Korthals (2008), 'Sincerity, Reliability and Other Ironies – Notes on Dave Eggers' *A Heartbreaking Work of Staggering Genius*', in Elke D'hoker and Gunther Martens (eds), *Narrative Unreliability in the Twentieth-Century First-Person Novel*. Berlin: Walter de Gruyter, 107–128.

Altieri, Charles (2009), 'Why Modernist Claims for Autonomy Matter', *Journal of Modern Literature* 3, 1–21.

Attridge, Derek (2004a), *The Singularity of Literature*. New York: Routledge.

Attridge, Derek (2004b), *J. M. Coetzee and the Ethics of Reading*. Chicago: University of Chicago Press.

Attridge, Derek (2015), *The Work of Literature*. Oxford: Oxford University Press.

Auden, Wystan Hugh (2015), *The Enchafèd Flood: Or the Romantic Iconography of the Sea*. London: Forgotten Books.

Beiser, Frederick C. (2003), *The Romantic Imperative: The Concept of Early German Romanticism*. Cambridge, MA: Harvard University Press.

Benjamin, Walter (1996), *The Concept of Criticism in German Romanticism*. Selected Writings, Vol. 1: 1913-1926. Cambridge, MA: Harvard University Press. Translation of *Der Begriff der Kunstkritik in der deutschen Romantik*. Kritische Gesamtausgabe. Band 3. Frankfurt a/M: Suhrkamp, 1920.

Bennett, Tony (2010), 'Sociology, Aesthetics, Expertise', *New Literary History* 41, 253-76.

Berlin, Isaiah (1999), *The Roots of Romanticism*. London: Chatto & Windus.

Blanchot, Maurice (1982), *The Space of Literature*. Lincoln: University of Nebraska Press. Translation of *L'Espace littéraire*. Paris: Gallimard, 1955.

Blanchot, Maurice (1993), *The Infinite Conversation*. Minneapolis: University of Minnesota Press. Translation of *L'Entretien infini*. Paris: Gallimard, 1969.

Blanchot, Maurice (1995), *The Work of Fire*. Stanford: Stanford University Press. Translation of *La Part du feu*. Paris: Gallimard, 1949.

Booth, Wayne C. (1989), *The Company We Keep: An Ethics of Fiction*. Berkeley: University of California Press.

Bourdieu, Pierre (1984), *Distinction: A Social Critique on the Judgment of Taste*. New York: Routledge. Translation of *La Distinction: Critique sociale du jugement*. Paris: Minuit, 1979.

Bourdieu, Pierre (2003), *Firing Back: Against the Tyranny of the Market 2*. New York: Verso. Translation of *Contre-feux 2: Pour un mouvement social européen*. Paris: Raisons d'agir, 2001.

Bourriaud, Nicolas (1999), *Formes de vie: L'art moderne et l'invention de soi*. Paris: Denoël.

Bourriaud, Nicolas (2002), *Relational Aesthetics*. Dijon: Les Presses du réel. Translation of *Esthétique relationnelle*. Dijon: Les Presses du réel, 1998.

Bourriaud, Nicolas (2005), *Postproduction: Culture as Screenplay – How Art Reprogrammes the World*. New York: Lukas & Sternberg. Translation of *Postproduction: La culture comme scénario – Comment l'art reprogramme le monde contemporain*. Dijon: Les presses du réel, 2002.

Bourriaud, Nicolas (2009a), *The Radicant*. New York: Sternberg. Translation of *Radicant: Pour une esthétique de la globalisation*. Paris: Denoël, 2009.

Bourriaud, Nicolas (2009b), 'Precarious Constructions: Answer to Jacques Rancière on Art and Politics', *Open* 17, 1-8.

Brandom, Robert, ed. (2000), *Rorty and His Critics*. Oxford: Blackwell.

Brooks, Cleanth (1957), 'Implications of an Organic Theory of Poetry', in M.H. Abrams (ed.), *Literature and Belief: English Institute Essay*. New York: Columbia University Press.

Brown, Marshall (1993), 'Romanticism and Enlightenment', in *The Cambridge Companion to British Romanticism*. Cambridge: Cambridge University Press.

Brown, Marshall (2000), *The Cambridge History of Literary Criticism, Vol. V: Romanticism*. Cambridge: Cambridge University Press.

Bruyne, Paul De and Pascal Gielen, eds (2011), *Community Art: The Politics of Trespassing*. Amsterdam: Valiz.

Butler, Stella (2009), 'A Manifesto for Positive Aesthetics: Review of Rita Felski, *Uses of Literature*', *Online Journal of Literary Theory*.

Carroll, Noël (2010), 'At the Crossroads of Ethics and Aesthetics', *Philosophy and Literature* 34, 248–59.

Casanova, Pascale (2004), *The World Republic of Letters*. Cambridge, MA: Harvard University Press.

Cassange, Albert (1906), *Théorie de l'art pour l'art chez les derniers romantiques et les premiers réalistes*. Seyssel: Editions Champ Vallon.

Compagnon, Antoine (2007), *Littérature, pour quoi faire?* Paris: Fayard/ Collège de France.

'Context?' (2011), [Special Issue], *New Literary History* 42:4.

Critchley, Simon (1992), *The Ethics of Deconstruction: Derrida and Levinas*. Oxford: Blackwell.

Dalrymple, Theodor (2005), *Our Culture, What's Left of It: The Mandarins and the Masses*. Chicago: Ivan R. Dee.

Danto, Arthur (1964), 'The Artworld', *Journal of Philosophy* 61, 571–84.

Deleuze, Gilles and Claire Parnet (1987), *Dialogues*. London: The Athlone Press. Translation of *Dialogues*. Paris: Flammarion, 1977.

Deleuze, Gilles and Felix Guattari (2004), *A Thousand Plateaus: Capitalism and Schizophrenia*. New York: Continuum. Translation of *Mille Plateaux: Capitalisme et schizophrénie*. Paris: Minuit, 1980.

Derrida, Jacques (1995), 'Passions: An Oblique Offering', in *On the Name*. Stanford: Stanford University Press. Translation of *Passions*. Paris: Galilée, 1993.

Devisch, Ignaas (2012), *Jean-Luc Nancy and the Question of Community*. New York: Bloomsbury.

D'hoker, Elke and Gunther Martens, eds (2008), *Narrative Unreliability in the Twentieth-Century First-Person Novel*. Berlin: Walter de Gruyter.

Dickie, George (1974), *Art and the Aesthetic: An Institutional Analysis*. Ithaca, NY: Cornell University Press.

Doorman, Maarten (2004), *De romantische orde*. Amsterdam: Bert Bakker.

Doorman, Maarten (2015), 'Persistent Autonomy and Romanticism', *Aesthetic Investigations* 1:1, 73–86.

Doyle, Jon (2018), 'The Changing Face of Post-Postmodern Fiction: Irony, Sincerity, and Populism', *Critique* 59:3, 259–70.

Dulk, Allard den (2015), *Existentialist Engagement in Wallace, Eggers and Foer: A Philosophical Analysis of Contemporary American Literature*. New York: Bloomsbury.

Duve, Thierry de (1998), *Kant after Duchamp*. Cambridge: MIT Press, 1998. Revised translation of *Au nom de l'art: Pour une archéologie de la modernité*. Paris: Minuit, 1988.

Eagleton, Terry (1990), *The Ideology of the Aesthetic*. Oxford: Blackwell.

Ellis, John Martin (1997), *Literature Lost: Social Agendas and the Corruption of the Humanities*. New Haven/London: Yale University Press.

Eyers, Tom (2017), 'Critical Response II: Theory over Method, or in Defense of Polemic', *Critical Inquiry* 44, Autumn, 136–43.

Felski, Rita (2008), *Uses of Literature*. Oxford: Blackwell.

Felski, Rita (2015), *The Limits of Critique*. Chicago: University of Chicago Press.

Fitzgerald, Jonathan D. (2012), 'Sincerity, Not Irony, Is Our Age's Ethos', *The Atlantic*, 20 November.

Foucault, Michel ([1970] 2004), *The Order of Things: An Archeology of the Human Sciences*. London: Routledge. Translation of *Les mots et les choses: Une archéologie des sciences humaines*. Paris: Gallimard, 1966.

Frank, Manfred (2004), *The Philosophical Foundations of Early German Romanticism*. New York: State University of New York Press. Translation of *Einführung in die frühromantische Ästhetik*. Frankfurt a/M: Suhrkamp, 1989.

Früchtl, Josef (2009), *The Impertinent Self: A Heroic History of Modernity*. Stanford: Stanford University Press. Translation of *Das unverschämte Ich: Eine Heldengeschichte der Moderne*. Frankfurt a/M: Suhrkamp, 2004.

Bibliography

Gadamer, Hans-Georg (1986), *The Relevance of Beauty, and Other Essays*. Cambridge: Cambridge University Press. Translation of *Die Aktualität des Schönen: Kunst als Spiel, Symbol und Fest*. Stuttgart: Reclam, 1977.

Gasché, Rudolphe (1999), *Of Minimal Things: Studies on the Notion of Relation*. Stanford: Stanford University Press.

Gielen, Pascal (2011), 'Mapping Community Art', in Paul De Bruyne and Pascal Gielen (eds), *Community Art: The Politics of Trespassing*. Amsterdam: Valiz.

Glissant, Édouard (1997), *Poetics of Relation*. Ann Arbor: University of Michigan Press. Translation of *Poétique de la relation*. Paris: Gallimard, 1990.

Goldstone, Andrew (2013), *Fictions of Autonomy: From Wilde to De Man*. Oxford: Oxford University Press.

Gumbrecht, Hans Ulrich (2012), *Atmosphere, Mood, Stimmung: On a Hidden Potential of Literature*. Stanford: Stanford University Press.

Hall, Donald E. (2004), *Subjectivity*. New York: Routledge.

Hardt, Michael and Antonio Negri (2009), *Common Wealth*. Cambridge, MA: The Belknap Press of Harvard University Press.

Heidegger, Martin (1985), *Schelling's Treatise on the Essence of Freedom*. Ohio: Ohio University Press. Translation of *Schelling: Vom Wesen der Menschlichen Freiheit*, 1809.

Heidegger, Martin (1997), *Der Deutsche Idealismus (Fichte, Hegel, Schelling) und die philosophische Problemlage der Gegenwart*. Frankfurt a/M: Vittorio Klostermann.

Heidegger, Martin (2000), *Elucidations of Hölderlin's Poetry*. Amherst, NY: Humanities Books. Translation of *Erläuterungen zu Hölderlins Dichtung*. Frankfurt a/M: Vittorio Klostermann, 1944.

Heinich, Nathalie (1996), *The Glory of Van Gogh: An Anthropology of Admiration*. Princeton: Princeton University Press. Translation of *La Gloire de Van Gogh: Essai d'anthropologie de l'admiration*. Paris: Minuit, 1991.

Heinich, Nathalie (2000), *Être écrivain: Création et identité*. Paris: Découverte.

Heumakers, Arnold (2004), 'Aesthetic Autonomy and Literary Commitment: A Pattern in Nineteenth-Century Literature', in Barend van Heusden and Liebeth Korthals Altes (eds), *Aesthetic Autonomy: Problems and Perspectives*. Leuven: Peeters, 21–36.

Hillis Miller, Joseph (2001), *Others*. Princeton: Princeton University Press.

Hillis Miller, Joseph (2002), *On Literature*. New York: Routledge.

Hirschorn, Michael (2011), 'Irony, The End of: Why Graydon Carter Wasn't Entirely Wrong', *New Yorker Magazine*, 27 August.

Hölderlin, Friedrich (1953), *Sämtliche Werke*. Band 2. Stuttgarter Ausgabe.

Holland, Mary K. (2014), *Succeeding Postmodernism: Language and Humanism in Contemporary American Literature*. New York: Bloomsbury.

Honour, Hugh (1991), *Romanticism*. Harmondsworth: Penguin Books.

Huber, Irmtraud (2014), *Literature after Postmodernism: Reconstructive Fantasies*. New York: Palgrave Macmillan.

James, Ian (2006), *The Fragmentary Demand: An Introduction to the Philosophy of Jean-Luc Nancy*. Stanford: Stanford University Press.

Jusdanis, Gregory (2005), 'Two Cheers for Aesthetic Autonomy', *Cultural Critique* 61, 22–54.

Jusdanis, Gregory (2010), *Fiction Agonistes: In Defense of Literature*. Stanford: Stanford University Press.

Kaiser, Birgit Mara (2012), *Figures of Simplicity: Sensation and Thinking in Kleist and Melville*. New York: State University of New York Press.

Kant, Immanuel (1991), *An Answer to the Question: What Is Enlightenment?* New York: Cambridge University Press. Translation of *Was heisst Aufklärung?*, 1784.

Kant, Immanuel (2000), *Critique of the Power of Judgment*. New York: Cambridge University Press. Translation of *Kritik der Urteilskraft*, 1790.

Kelly, Adam (2014), 'Dialectics of Sincerity: Lionel Trilling and David Foster Wallace', *Post45*, 17 October.

Kernan, Alvin (1990), *The Death of Literature*. New Haven/London: Yale University Press.

Kivy, Peter (2012), 'What Really Happened in the Eighteenth Century: The "Modern System" Re-examined (Again)', *British Journal of Aesthetics* 52:1, 61–74.

Konstantinou, Lee (2016), *Cool Characters*. Cambridge, MA: Harvard University Press.

Kramnick Jonathan and Anahid Nersessian (2017), 'Form and Explanation', *Critical Inquiry* 43, Spring, 650–69.

Kuhn, Thomas (1963), *The Structure of Scientific Revolutions*. Chicago: University of Chicago Press.

Kundera, Milan (1986), *The Art of the Novel*. New York: HarperCollins. Translation of *L'Art du roman*. Paris: Gallimard, 1986.

Lacoue-Labarthe, Philippe (1993), *The Subject of Philosophy*. Minneapolis: University of Minnesota Press. Translation of *Le sujet de la philosophie*. Paris: Flammarion, 1979.

Lacoue-Labarthe, Philippe (2007), *Heidegger and the Politics of Poetry*. Urbana: University of Illinois Press. Translation of *Heidegger: La politique du poème*. Paris: Galilée, 2000.

Lacoue-Labarthe, Philippe and Jean-Luc Nancy (1988), *The Literary Absolute: The Theory of Literature in German Romanticism*. New York: State University of New York Press. Translation of *L'Absolu littéraire: Théorie de la littérature du romantisme allemand*. Paris: Seuil, 1978.

Lakshmipathy, Vinod (2009), 'Kant and the Turn to Romanticism', *Kritike* 3:2, 90–102.

Landa, Manuel De (2006), *A New Philosophy of Society: Assemblage Theory and Social Complexity*. New York: Continuum.

Landsdown, Richard (2001), *The Autonomy of Literature*. Houndsmills: Macmillan.

Latour, Bruno (2005), *Reassembling the Social: An Introduction to Actor-Network-Theory*. Oxford: Oxford University Press.

Law, John and John Hassard, eds (1990), *Actor Network Theory and After*. Oxford: Blackwell.

LeBlanc, Charles et al. (2003), *La forme poétique du monde: Anthologie du romantisme allemand*. Paris: Éditions José Corti.

Levine, Caroline (2015), *Forms: Whole, Rhythm, Hierarchy, Network*. Princeton: Princeton University Press.

Levine, Caroline (2017), 'Critical Response I: Still Polemicizing after All These Years', *Critical Inquiry* 44, Autumn, 129–35.

Loesberg, Jonathan (2005), *A Return to Aesthetics: Autonomy, Indifference, and Postmodernism*. Stanford: Stanford University Press.

Mackenzie, Catriona and Nataliw Stoljar, eds (2000), *Relational Autonomy: Feminist Perspectives on Autonomy, Agency and the Social Self*. New York: Oxford University Press.

Magill, R. Jay, Jr. (2012a), *Sincerity: How a Moral Ideal Born Five Hundred Years Ago also Inspired Religious Wars, Modern Art....* New York: W.W. Norton & Company.

Magill, R. Jay, Jr. (2012b), 'We've Been Arguing about Sincerity vs. Irony for Millennia', *The Atlantic*, 26 November.

Marx, William (2005), *L'Adieu à la littérature: Histoire d'une dévalorisation, XVIIIe–XXe siècle*. Paris: Minuit, 2005.

McDonald, Ronan (2007), *Death of the Critic*. London: Continuum, 2007.

Morin, Marie-Eve (2012), *Jean-Luc Nancy*. Cambridge: Polity Press.

Moritz, Karl Philip (1962), 'Versuch einer Vereinigung aller schönen Künste und Wissenschaften unter dem Begriff des in sichselbst Vollendeten (1785)', in *Schriften zur Ästhetik und Poetik*. Tübingen: H.J. Schrimpf.

Nancy, Jean-Luc (1982), 'Sharing of Voices', in Gayle L. Ormiston and Alan D. Schrift (eds), *Transforming the Hermeneutic Context: From Nietzsche to Nancy*. New York: SUNY Press, 1989. Translation of *Le partage des voix*. Paris: Galilée, 1982.

Nancy, Jean-Luc (1991), *The Inoperative Community*. Minneapolis: University of Minnesota Press. Translation of *La communauté désœuvrée*. Paris: Bourgeois, 1986.

Nancy, Jean-Luc (1993), *The Experience of Freedom*. Stanford: Stanford University Press. Translation of *L'Expérience de la liberté*. Paris: Galilée, 1988.

Nancy, Jean-Luc (1997), *The Sense of the World*. Minneapolis: University of Minnesota Press. Translation of *Le sens du monde*. Paris: Galilée, 1993.

Nancy, Jean-Luc (2000), *Being Singular Plural*. Stanford: Stanford University Press. Translation of *Être singulier pluriel*. Paris: Galilée, 1996.

Nancy, Jean-Luc (2001), *The Muses*. Stanford: Stanford University Press. Translation of *Les muses*. Paris: Galilée, 1996.

Nancy, Jean-Luc (2007), *The Creation of the World, or Globalization*. New York: State University of New York Press. Translation of *La création du monde ou la mondialisation*, Paris: Galilée, 2002.

Nancy, Jean-Luc (2018), *Expectation: Philosophy, Literature*. New York: Fordham University Press. Translation of *Demande: Littérature et philosophie*, Paris: Galilée, 2015.

Nancy, Jean-Luc (2018), 'The Poet's Calculation', in Jean-Luc Nancy, *Expectation: Philosophy, Literature*. New York: Fordham University Press. 2018, 83–107.

Neill, Alex and Aaron Ridley (2012), 'Relational Theories of Art: The History of an Error', *British Journal of Aesthetics* 52:2, 141–51.

Nietzsche, Friedrich (2008), *The Birth of Tragedy Out of the Spirit of Music*. Oxford: Oxford University Press. Translation of *Die Geburt der Tragödie aus dem Geiste der Musik*, 1872.

Nussbaum, Martha (1992), *Love's Knowledge: Essays on Philosophy and Literature*. Oxford: Oxford University Press.

Nussbaum, Martha (2010), *Not for Profit: Why Democracy Needs the Humanities*. Princeton: Princeton University Press.

Ormiston, Gayle and Alan Schrift, eds (1989), *Transforming the Hermeneutic Context: From Nietzsche to Nancy*. New York: SUNY Press.

Posner, Richard A. (2002), *Public Intellectuals: A Study of Decline*. Cambridge, MA: Harvard University Press.

Praz, Mario (1970), *The Romantic Agony*. Oxford: Oxford University Press.

Punter, David (2003), 'Romanticism', in Martin Coyle et al. (eds), *Encyclopedia of Literature and Criticism*. New York: Routledge.

Rancière, Jacques (1991), *The Ignorant Schoolmaster: Five Lessons in Intellectual Emancipation*. Stanford: Stanford University Press. Translation of *Le maître ignorant: Cinq leçons sur l'émancipation intellectuelle*. Paris: Fayard, 1987.

Rancière, Jacques (2002), 'The Aesthetic Revolution and Its Outcomes: Emplotments of Autonomy and Heteronomy', *New Left Review* 14, 133–51.

Rancière, Jacques (2004a), *The Philosopher and His Poor*. Durham: Duke University Press. Translation of *Le philosophe et ses pauvres*. Paris: Fayard, 1983.

Rancière, Jacques (2004b), *The Politics of Aesthetics: Distribution of the Sensible*. New York: Bloomsbury. Translation of *Le Partage du sensible: Esthétique et politique*. Paris: La Fabrique, 2000.

Rancière, Jacques (2007), *The Future of the Image*. New York: Verso Books. Translation of *Le destin des images*. Paris: La Fabrique, 2003.

Rancière, Jacques (2009), *The Emancipated Spectator*. New York: Verso Books. Translation of *Le spectateur émancipé*. Paris: La Fabrique, 2008.

Rancière, Jacques (2010), *Dissensus: On Politics and Aesthetics*. New York: Continuum.

Rancière, Jacques (2011a), *Mute Speech: Literature, Critical Theory and Politics*. New York: Columbia University Press. Translation of *La parole muette: Essai sur les contradictions de la littérature*. Paris: Hachette, 1998.

Rancière, Jacques (2011b), *The Politics of Literature*. Cambridge: Polity Press. Translation of *Politique de la littérature*. Paris: Galilée, 2007.

Rancière, Jacques (2013), *Aisthesis: Scenes from the Aesthetic Regime of Art*. New York: Verso Books. Translation of *Aisthesis: Scènes du régime esthétique de l'art*. Paris: Galilée, 2011.

Ricoeur, Paul (1970), *Freud and Philosophy: An Essay on Interpretation*. New Haven/London: Yale University Press. Translation of *De l'interprétation: Essai sur Sigmund Freud*. Paris: Seuil, 1965.

Rooden, Aukje van (2009), 'Poésie haptique: Sur l'(ir)réalité du toucher poétique chez Nancy', *Revue Philosophique de Louvain* 107:1, 127–42.

Rooden, Aukje van (2010), *L'Intrigue dénouée: Politique et littérature dans une communauté sans mythes*. Doctoral dissertation, Tilburg University, the Netherlands.

Rooden, Aukje van (2012), 'Magnifying *The Mirror and the Lamp*: A Critical Reconsideration of the Abramsian Poetical Model and Its Contribution to the Research of Modern Dutch Literature', *Journal of Dutch Literature* 3:1, 65–87.

Rooden, Aukje van (2015a), 'Reconsidering Literary Autonomy: From an Individual towards a Relational Paradigm', *Journal of the History of Ideas* 76:2, 167–90.

Rooden, Aukje van (2015b), 'Our Engagement with Literature: On Literature as a Way of Being', *Journal of Dutch Literature* 6:1, 59–67.

Rorty, Richard (1989), *Contingency, Irony, and Solidarity*. Cambridge: Cambridge University Press.

Rosenblatt, Roger (2001), 'The Age of Irony Comes to an End', *Time Magazine*, 24 September.

Rutten, Ellen (2017), *Sincerity after Communism: A Cultural History*. New Haven/London: Yale University Press.

Safranski, Rüdiger (2004), *Schiller oder die Erfindung des deutchen Idealismus*. München: Carl Hanser Verlag.

Safranski, Rüdiger (2014), *Romanticism: A German Affair*. Evanston: Northwestern University Press. Translation of *Romantik: Eine deutsche Affäre*. München: Carl Hanser Verlag, 2007.

Sartre, Jean-Paul (1988), *'What Is Literature?' and Other Essays*. Cambridge, MA: Harvard University Press. Translation of *Qu'est-ce que la littérature?* Paris: Gallimard, 1948.

Schlegel, Friedrich (1968), *Dialogue on Poetry and Literary Aphorisms*. University Park: Pennsylvania State University Press.

Schlegel, Friedrich (1971), *Friedrich Schlegel's Lucinde and the Fragments*. Minneapolis: University of Minnesota Press. Selection translated from Friedrich Schlegel, *Kritische Friedrich Schlegel Ausgabe*. Band 2. München/Paderborn: F. Schöningh, 1967.

Schleiermacher, Friedrich (1998), *Hermeneutics and Criticism, and Other Writings*. Cambridge: Cambridge University Press. Translation of *Hermeneutik und Kritik*. Frankfurt a/M: Suhrkamp, 1993.

Schiller, Friedrich (1879), *Sämmtliche Werke*. Band 4. Stuttgart: J.G. Cotta'sche Buchhandlung.

Schiller, Friedrich (2004), *On the Aesthetic Education of Man*. New York: Dover Publications. Translation of *Über die ästhetische Erziehung des Menschen* [1794–5].

Seigel, Jerrold (2005), *The Idea of the Self: Thought and Experience in Western Europe since the Seventeenth Century*. Cambridge: Cambridge University Press.

Spivak, Gayatri Chakravorty (2003), *Death of a Discipline*. New York: Columbia University Press.

Stinson, Emmett (2017), *Satirizing Modernism: Aesthetic Autonomy, Romanticism, and the Avant-Garde*. New York: Bloomsbury.

Taylor, Charles (1975), *Hegel*. Cambridge: Cambridge University Press.

Taylor, Charles (1989), *Sources of the Self: The Making of Modern Identity*. Cambridge, MA: Harvard University Press.

Thacker, Eugene (2009), 'Review of Alberto Toscano, *The Theatre of Production: Philosophy and Individuation between Kant and Deleuze*', *Parrhesia* 7, 86–91.

Timmer, Nicoline (2010), *Do You Feel It Too? The Post-Postmodern Syndrome in American Fiction at the Turn of the Millennium*. Amsterdam: Rodopi.

Todorov, Tzvetan (2007), *La littérature en péril*. Paris: Flammarion.

Tönnies, Ferdinand (2001), *Community and Civil Society*. Cambridge: Cambridge University Press. Translation of *Gemeinschaft und Gesellschaft: Grundbegriffe der reinen Soziologie*. Darmstadt: Wissenschaftliche Buchgesellschaft, 1979.

Toscano, Alberto (2006), *The Theatre of Production: Philosophy and Individuation from Kant to Deleuze*. London: Palgrave Macmillan.

Vaessens, Thomas and Yra van Dijk, eds (2011), *Reconsidering the Postmodern: European Literature beyond Relativism*. Amsterdam: Amsterdam University Press.

Varela Francisco, Evan Thompson and Eleanor Rosch (1991), *The Embodied Mind: Cognitive Science and Human Experience*. Cambridge: MIT Press.

Vermeulen, Timotheus and Robin van den Akker(2010), 'Notes on Metamodernism', *Journal of Aesthetics and Culture* 2, 1–14.

Voelz, Johannes (2016), 'The New Sincerity as Literary Hospitality', in Jeffrey Clapp and Emily Ridge (eds), *Security and Hospitality in Literature and Culture*. New York: Routledge.

Walhout, Donald (1996), 'The Hermeneutical Turn in American Critical Theory, 1830–1860', *Journal of the History of Ideas* 57:4, 683–703.

Weitz, Morris (1956), 'The Role of Theory in Aesthetics', *Journal of Aesthetics and Art Criticism* 15, 27–35.

Williams, Zoe (2003), 'The Final Irony', *The Guardian*, 28 June.

Wellek, René (1949), 'The Concept of "Romanticism" in Literary History', *Comparative Literature* 1, 1–23.

Wolosky, Shira (2010), 'Relational Aesthetics and Feminist Poetics', *New Literary History* 41:3, 571–91.

Wood, David W., ed. (2004), *Novalis: Notes for a Romantic Encyclopedia – Das Algemeine Brouillon*. New York: State University of New York Press.

Woodmansee, Martha (1996), *The Author, Art, and the Market: Rereading the History of Aesthetics*. New York: Columbia University Press.

Wordsworth, William (1974), 'Advertisement to *Lyrical Ballads* (1798)', in Warwick Jack Burgoyne Owen and Jane Worthington Smyser (eds), *Prose Works of William Wordsworth*. Oxford: Clarendon Press.

Index

Abrams, M. H. 27–8, 33, 73–7, 92
   expressive poetics 27–9, 35,
     73–6, 124 n.5
   mimetic poetics 58, 73–6
   objective poetics 73–5, 77
   pragmatic poetics 73–6
Adorno, Theodor 12–14, 17, 73,
    83–6, 136 n.6.
aesthetics 5, 13, 18, 24, 64, 90, 93,
   98, 114
   aesthetic education
    (Schiller) 36–8, 47, 50, 60,
    62, 64, 125 n.22
   aesthetic judgement (Kant) 9,
    18, 41–2, 61, 78, 98, 102
   aesthetic regime (Rancière)
    25–6, 71–2, 84, 136 n.5, 137 n.8
   Aesthetic Theory (Adorno)
    12–13, 17
   vs. ethics 105–8
   relational aesthetics (see under
    relationality)
   Romantic aesthetics 21, 24, 78, 86
antagonism 83–5, 91
   antagonistic 21, 64, 73, 83–4, 91
anti-autonomism 1, 7, 16, 72–3,
   78, 83–4
anti-autonomization 72
anti-autonomist (adjective) 2,
   6–7, 17–20, 64–5, 67, 69, 72, 83
anti-autonomist (person) 5, 7,
   9–10, 15, 17–18, 48–9, 64, 69,
   95, 103
anti-worldliness 5, 50
apolitical 6
art-pour-l'art, l' 16, 64–5, 67–8, 72
   art for art's sake 67–9, 132 n.27
   art pour l'art debate, *l'* 65,
    68–9, 76

Athenaeum 31, 33–4, 44, 46, 59,
   126 n.22
Augier, Émile 66
autonomization 7, 10, 15, 49, 51,
   67, 72–3
autonomism 6, 16, 72–3, 77–8, 83
   vs. anti-autonomism 16, 72–3,
    78, 83
autonomist (adjective) 17–20,
   64–5, 72, 83, 86, 117
autonomist (person) 8, 15,
   17–18, 48, 64, 69, 95, 103,
   114–15, 117–18
autonomy 1–3, 8, 10, 11–13,
   15, 17–18, 20, 22, 40–3,
   48–50, 55, 60–1, 63, 71–3,
   78, 79–81, 84–5, 99, 105–6,
   108, 110, 115. See also self-
   regulation
   aesthetic autonomy 9, 15,
    17, 79
   literary autonomy 1–2, 5, 7–12,
    16–19, 21, 26, 31, 39, 49–50,
    62, 71, 79, 85, 93, 113
   autonomy debate 1, 6, 13, 16–17,
    117
avant-garde 64, 79, 101, 132 n.16

Balzac, Honoré de 85, 98
Barthes, Roland 2, 56
Baudelaire, Charles 63
Bildung 27, 33, 36, 43, 105
Blanc, Louis 66
Blanchot, Maurice 93, 100–1,
   109–10
Bourdieu, Pierre 2, 8–12, 14, 67, 86
bourgeoisie 65–6, 70
   bourgeois writers 65–8, 72,
    135 n.52

Index

Bourriaud, Nicolas 90–3, 97, 109, 139 n.21, 140 n.29
Carroll, Noël 17
Cassange, Albert 67–8
Coleridge, Samuel Taylor 77–8, 134 n.46
commitment 5, 11, 15, 22, 103, 108, 115. See also engagement
 vs. autonomy 3, 20, 48, 108, 113–14
 committed 4, 91, 103
 literary commitment 16, 72, 85, 103
 social commitment 4, 85, 103
context 57, 75–80, 87–8, 90, 117
 contextualism 16, 90, 138 n.15
 vs. text 73–9, 90, 114, 134 nn.47, 48, 138 n.15
creativity 24, 27, 31, 34–5, 42
Cousin, Victor 65, 72
Cultural Studies 87, 89

Dalrymple, Theodor (a.k.a. Anthony M. Daniels) 3
deconstructivism 57
 deconstructivist 109, 131 n.6
De Duve, Thierry 98–9, 116
Deleuze, Gilles 57
derealization. See under reality
Derrida, Jacques 57, 93, 98
De Saussure, Ferdinand 56
detachment 4–5, 50, 103. See also disengagement
determinism 3
 deterministic 3, 16, 73
dialectic 16
 dialectical 55
disengagement 4, 49–50. See also detachment
disinterested 5, 11
disinterestness 18
Doorman, Maarten 24, 123 n.2

Dostoyevsky, Fyodor 57, 102
dualism 49, 81, 92, 113–14, 129 n.51, 143 n.52
dualist 61, 73–4, 81, 90, 115
Duchamp, Marchel 98–9

Eagleton, Terry 71, 133 n.34
Eggers, Dave 3, 14
engagement 4–5, 49, 90, 112, 114, 141 n.41. See also disengagement
 littérature engagée 4
Enlightenment 27, 35–6, 38–40, 53–4, 56–7, 80, 86, 124 n.5
épistémè 24–5
ethics (vs. aesthetics) 91, 105–6, 108, 114
 ethical 14, 16, 26, 89, 91, 103–7, 109, 142 nn.48, 52
 ethical regime (Rancière) 25
existentialism 56, 64, 80
expression (personal, emotional) 19, 25, 27–8, 30, 32–3, 35, 44, 48–9, 51
expressive poetics (see under Abrams, M.H.)

Felski, Rita 4–6
feminism 57
Fitzgerald, Jonathan D. 3
flarf poetry 99
Flaubert, Gustave 63, 85, 98
forgetfulness of literature 20, 86, 88, 116
formalism 7, 16. See also New Formalism
Foucault, Michel 24–5, 54, 57, 131 n.7
French Revolution 36, 38, 53, 55
Friedrich, Caspar David 27
Früchtl, Josef 70, 131 n.6
futurism 60, 68

Gautier, Théophile   65, 72
genius   24, 27–30, 32, 35, 124 n.12
Goldstone, Andrew   8, 17, 79, 133 n.30
Gumbrecht, Hans Ulrich   64, 138 n.15

Hall, Donald E.   56
Hegel, Georg Wilhelm Friedrich   10, 54–5
Heidegger, Martin   53, 56, 80–2, 84
Heinich, Nathalie   33
hermeneutic turn   57–9, 75, 131 nn.15, 16, 138 n.15
hermeneutics/hermeneutical approach   59, 116
heteronomy (vs. autonomy)   20–2, 41–3, 48–9, 54, 60–1, 63, 65, 72–3, 78, 80–1, 84, 129 n.51, 135 n.54, 139 n.1
heteronomous   42, 55, 62–3, 66, 82
Hölderlin, Friedrich   31, 53, 59, 126 n.22
Hugo, Victor   65

individuality   19, 31, 33, 44–6, 48, 53, 58, 70–1, 89, 95–6, 114. See also undivided
individual   19, 30–1, 34–5, 37–9, 42, 45–50, 57, 60, 62, 65, 70, 73, 95–6, 126 n.29, 140 n.29
individualization   30, 37
individuum   31
indivisable, indivisability   31
qualitative vs. quantitative   70–1
inner (self, soul, life)   28–9, 32, 35, 37, 45, 49, 57, 111
Irigaray, Luce   57
irony   3–5, 14, 59
ironic   13, 15
vs. sincerity   3, 14

Jusdanis, Gregory   8, 15, 17, 79, 84

Kafka, Franz   12, 84
Kant, Immanuel   29, 35–6, 39–43, 48–50, 54–5, 60–1, 63, 66, 70, 77, 80–1, 93, 95, 98
Critique of Pratical Reason   40
Critique of Pure Reason   40
Critique of the Power of Judgment   4–5, 29, 40, 63
Kristeva, Julia   57

Lacan, Jacques   56
Lacoue-Labarthe, Philippe   34
Levine, Caroline   6–7, 122 n.53, 138 n.15
literature. See also forgetfulness of literature
literary autonomy (see under autonomy)
literary commitment   16, 72, 103
literary history/historian   1–2, 16, 21, 50, 62, 67, 72–3, 130 n.55
Literary Studies   20, 22, 64, 73, 78–9, 87, 116, 134 n.47
literary theory   4–5, 8, 15–16, 21, 23, 49–50, 62, 73–5, 77, 113
as a mode of being   20, 88–90, 92–5, 97–8, 101, 110–11, 113, 116
Loesberg, Jonathan   8, 17, 61, 77, 98
Lyotard, François   57, 93

Magill, R. Jay   13–14
Mallarmé, Stéphane   71
Marx, Karl   54–6, 137 n.9
Marx, William   2–3, 5–7, 67, 72
metamodernism   4
mode of being, literature as. See under literature
modernity   15, 30, 53, 60, 66, 70–3, 76, 80, 82, 86, 90–1, 101, 111, 115, 131 n.6, 135 n.52
the notion of   71–2, 133 n.39
two forms of/Janus-faced   19, 53, 64, 70–3, 82, 90–2, 115, 143 n.52

Index

Nabokov, Vladimir 14, 105–6
Nancy, Jean-Luc 20, 34, 57, 93–7, 111, 139 n.23
Nerval, Gérard de 65
New Criticism 73–5, 78, 115, 134 n.46
New Formalism 6, 115
New Historicism 79, 87
New Sincerity 3–4, 13, 16
Nietzsche, Friedrich 54, 56
Novalis 29, 32, 47, 53, 96
Nussbaum, Martha 104, 108, 112

ontology 93, 114
  ontic 87–100, 103–4, 106–8, 110, 112
  ontological (approach) 20, 81, 86–90, 92–4, 99–101, 108–10, 112–14, 138 n.15
  nominalist ontology 99
organic (unity) 44, 46–7, 58, 77, 81, 97
organicism 77
organon 34
Orwell, George 90, 106

Pamuk, Orhan 110–12
paradigm. *See also* épistémè
  relational paradigm 20–1, 83, 86–7, 89, 93, 95–7, 102, 104, 108, 112–17, 137 n.14, 138 n.15, 140 n.31, 142 n.48
  Romantic paradigm 19–21, 23–8, 30–5, 37, 39, 43–5, 53–4, 57, 60–4, 72, 77–8, 80, 88–9, 95–6, 114, 132 n.22, 140 n.31
Plato 15
polemics/polemical debate 63, 65, 67–9, 72–3, 76, 89, 115
politics 8, 11, 91, 106. *See also* apolitical
  political 1, 4–5, 9, 11–12, 25, 36, 40, 66, 90–3, 97, 104, 106, 135 n.52

politics of depoliticization (Bourdieu) 11
socio-political 14, 26, 56, 76, 84, 88
Ponsard, François 66
post-colonial 79
post-modernism 16
  post-modern(ist) 16, 80, 101
  post-modernity 80
post-postmodernism 4, 13, 120 n.15
post-Romanticism 62
  post-Romantic 15, 21, 62–4, 71–3, 75, 77–8, 85, 114
post-structuralism 57
post-structuralist 54, 93, 109, 113
precariousness 109
  precarious 92, 97
Proudhon, Pierre-Joseph 66
psychoanalysis 56

Rancière, Jacques 24–6, 60–1, 71–2, 80, 83–6, 90–1, 98, 129 nn.51, 54, 136 n.6
reality 7, 12, 14, 25, 59, 75–6, 79, 84, 88–9, 97, 99–101, 109–10, 112
  de-realization 100, 102, 109
regime 25–6, 30. *See also* épistémè
  aesthetic regime (*see under* aesthetics)
  regime of singularity (Heinich) 30
relationality 81, 83, 87, 89–92, 94–7, 103, 114, 135 n.54, 138 n.15
relational aesthetics (Bourriaud) 90–3, 139 n.21
relational paradigm (*see under* paradigm)
relational turn 86
Romanticism 2, 4, 8, 16, 19, 21, 23, 36, 39–40, 44, 48–51, 59–60, 62, 69–70, 73–7, 79–80, 82, 89, 117
  Dutch Romanticism 69
  English Romanticism 29, 51, 7

French Romanticism 51, 65–8, 72
German Romanticism 19, 21, 31, 34, 36, 54, 58, 65, 72
Romantic aesthetics (*see under* aesthetics)
Romantic paradigm (*see under* paradigm)
Rorty, Richard 104–8, 112, 142 nn.48, 49
Rosenblatt, Roger 4

Safranski, Rüdiger 23–4, 59
Saint-Simon 65
Saint-Simonism 64
sapere aude 37
Sartre, Jean-Paul 2, 56, 71–2, 141 n.41
Schiller, Friedrich 60–2, 64, 72, 125 n.22, 126 n.29
Schlegel, Friedrich and/or Anton Wilhelm 31, 35, 43, 45–6, 53, 59
Schleiermacher, Friedrich 58–9
Seigel, Jerrold 87
self-regulation 1, 49. *See also* autonomy
sincerity 3, 7, 14
situatedness 80–1
socialist 13, 64, 66, 69
social relevance 7, 14, 18, 97, 103–4, 106–9, 112, 140 n.31, 141 n.36
social commitment 4, 85
social engagement 114
social fact (*fait social*) (Adorno) 13
social value 2, 5, 16, 104

sociology of literature 8, 30, 78, 87, 89, 115, 134 n.47
Stinson, Emmett 7, 79
structuralism 56–7
subjectivity 30, 38, 48–9, 55, 57, 80
subjective 27, 32–3, 51
symbol 94–5, 97
symbolic force (Adorno) 12
symbolisation (Nancy) 95, 97

Taylor, Charles 55, 58
text (*vs.* context) 50, 73–80, 90, 113–15, 117, 134 n.47, 138 n.15
Todorov, Tzvetan 6, 108
Tönnies, Ferdinand 70
Toscano, Alberto 81, 135 n.54
truth 54, 58–60, 75–6, 80, 83, 104, 132 n.16

undivided 19, 30–1, 35, 37, 39, 44–9, 57–9, 77, 89, 97. *See also* individuality
universality 35, 70
universal 32, 34, 38, 43–4, 103–4, 106, 142 n.48

vacuum, theoretical 19–20, 27, 51, 63
Van Gogh, Theo 30
Von Augustenburg, Friedrich Christiaan 36
Von Freytag-Loringhoven, Elsa 99

Wordsworth, William 28, 33

Zola, Émile 63

www.ingramcontent.com/pod-product-compliance
Lightning Source LLC
Chambersburg PA
CBHW052049300426
44117CB00012B/2049